Sweetness

and Light

Words and Visions

From the Journal of Patty Schmid

SWEETNESS AND LIGHT

ACKNOWLEDGEMENTS

Special blessings and thanks to the people whose lives have touched mine and enhanced the pages of this book...

Barb Boswell, who gave me a jump start on the book by typing from two of my journals.

Walter and Cathy Fleming, for the tireless work they did formatting and printing the first two drafts of this book. It was invaluable and encouraging to see my book in print and to hold it in my hand.

Ginger Rogers, for sharing her grammar skills and spending many hours editing this book with me. Her enthusiasm for the message kept me going.

John Schmid, my dear husband, for patience with me during the writing and editing process, and for rescuing my files when my hard drive crashed. He knows he's my hero!

CONTENTS

Introduction

How do I hear God's voice? What does it sound like?

I hear with my inner or spiritual sense of hearing. I have been a Christian for 40 years, but until 2007 I rarely heard God's voice, or if I did, I didn't recognize it. Many times He spoke to me through the written word, but hearing God speak in my spirit is something relatively new to me. It has changed my life and deepened my relationship with God.

In August 2007, my husband John and I attended a conference for our missions agency World Indigenous Missions. The main speaker was Mark Burlinson from Shiloh Place Ministries. He spoke about the Father's love, and in one of the sessions – "Steps to Intimacy with the Father" – he outlined how to listen to God's voice.

1. Quiet yourself (Ps. 46:10: "Be still and know that I am God")

2. Focus on Father God or Jesus

3. Tune into the spontaneous flow of thoughts that bubble up from within.

4. Write down what you "hear" (journaling)

Using this method, I started listening and journaling the very next morning. At first, it was a great effort to be still and to quiet myself and to focus on God. Amazingly, after a few minutes, I sensed God saying to me, "Patty, My child, I love you. I have a plan for your life,

Introduction

for today. Do you want to walk in it? Don't hide. I am light and in Me is no darkness. Walk in My light. If you let My light shine on your darkness, it will have to flee."

What does God's voice sound like? He speaks in my spirit and with an inner voice, so He sounds just like me when I talk to myself. Recently, someone explained this more clearly for me. If you count to 10 to yourself, what does it sound like? That's what God sounds like; He uses your inner voice. It's more than a thought; it is thoughts put into words.

Every day God tells me "I love you." I'm starting to believe it now. His love is amazing, and He tells me that I still have almost no idea how great His love is for me. Early in my times of listening to Him, He started calling me by a pet name, "Sweetness" or "Sweetness and Light". I was surprised at first, but it makes sense that a loving father would have pet names for his little children. God's love for us is the love of a father. When I come to Him as a little girl, He often calls me "Baby Girl" or "Princess."

After about a year of listening and journaling, in 2008, I discovered a workbook by Mark Virkler entitled "How to Hear God's Voice." As I started to study this book, it really helped me to go deeper in this journey and also gave me so much scriptural basis for what I was already doing. Then I got to the chapter on vision. Wow.... I am a visual learner, and being able to see what God wants me to see has had such an impact on me. I started seeing visions on a regular basis. I highly recommend "How to Hear God's Voice" to anyone who would like to get closer to God.

In this book I have included almost all the visions I have received so far. Many are personal, but I felt they were to be shared. When I say

Introduction

visions, the ones that I have are the ordinary kind. God uses my imagination, and the vision is on the screen of my mind. So far I have never seen anything really clearly, but I am able to describe the details the Lord wants me to see as I keep looking at the visions He gives me. To make it easier for the reader to see when I'm talking about a vision, in this book I have preceded visions with ** (double asterisk). Often I am able to come back to a vision and see more. For most of these visions, I have put the entries together to make it easier to read; I then continued with my journal entries in a chronological format.

I have written in quotes what I hear God speaking to me, and I added, "God says." Please know that these words are what I sense God is speaking to me, and although many of the words are based on scripture, they are not scripture, and as such are not meant to be used for doctrine. And, of course, because I am not perfect, I do not always hear perfectly. Sometimes, when what God says to me is directly based on scripture, I have included the reference in parenthesis. As a rule, God speaks to me in heart language, and His words to me build me up spiritually, emotionally, even physically. If there's something here that you don't think God would say to you, just pass over it. I hope you will be encouraged to hear God's voice for yourself.

I suggest you take this book at a slower pace, maybe reading two or three entries a day during your time of prayer with the Lord. Each of the journal entries here took several minutes, sometimes even more than an hour for me to receive. You could think about what God has said to me and then ask Him, "What are You saying to me today?" When you read the visions God has given me, think about what it means and ask God to show you what it means. I encourage you to start your own journal if you haven't already.

3

Introduction

I no longer have to be alone in order to hear God's voice. If I stop and quiet myself and focus on Jesus, I can hear Him speak to me even when I'm in a crowd. I can hear Him right now. He says, "I love you, I'm with you, and I'm here to help you." After four years of journaling, I have filled 14 notebooks of various shapes and sizes. God continues to speak to me every day, and I write sometimes just a paragraph, sometimes pages. I have included here only highlights. God assures me, "The best is yet to come!"

Father Sings Over Me

Chapter 1

Father Sings Over Me

Draw Near

"Sweetness," Father says, "this is the most important thing you ever do – you must make time to listen to Me. If you don't, you will miss out on what I have for you. I forgive you for not coming to Me first this morning. It's so important that you learn to obey My gentle leadings. I choose to speak to you in the still, small voice in your spirit. I won't override your will. I cleanse you from that failure to obey. If you obey and draw near to Me, you will hear My voice more clearly."

(I hear God singing over Me in this song.)

DRAW NEAR

Draw near to Me, My love/ Draw near to Me, My fair one

Precious, you are precious to Me/ Your love to Me is sweet

I love these times when you draw near

And you can receive My love

Draw near to Me My child/ I pour My love out on you

Why did you wait so long to come?

I could have helped you/ I could have held you in My arms

Father Sings Over Me

Draw near, now come here

I will hold you, I will love you

I will hold you in My arms

Precious, you are precious to Me

I'm holding you, I'm loving you/ I'm holding you in My arms

Confidence

"Hello, Sweetness," Father assures me, "I'm here with you. I love you; you are Mine. I want to fill you with My confidence, confidence in Me and My love for you, confidence in who you are. You are a princess in My house, seated with Me in heavenly places. You have boldness and confident access to Me because of what Jesus did, Daughter (Eph 3:12). Draw near with a sincere heart in full assurance of faith (Heb 10:22). Draw near because you are washed and clean. Draw near with confidence to My throne of grace – you will receive mercy and grace to help in time of need (Heb 4:16). You always need My help, Beloved. Abide in Me, and your confidence will <u>grow</u>. Your confidence comes from Me; I want to fill you with it (2 Cor. 3:5). I am able to do exceeding abundantly above all you ask or think according to the power, My power that works within you (Eph. 3:20). My Holy Spirit works within you – the same Spirit that raised Jesus Christ from the dead (Rom 8:11). My Spirit brings life, health, healing and blessing to you and your body. I love you, and My love fills you with confidence now. You are My daughter; you can cry out, "Daddy" whenever you need help, and you always need help (Rom 8:15-16). Hold your head high in confidence and look up, for I am holding your hand. I gave you My own Son, and I will freely give you ALL THINGS

Father Sings Over Me

(Rom 8:32). You are My precious daughter, My little baby girl, and I love you."

"I'm writing My words on the tablet of your heart, words of love and beauty, special words for you alone," Father says. "Precious One, draw near so I may fill you more. You need more of My love. I love you, Precious One. I'm here with you. There's ALWAYS more for you to receive. My love is extravagant—more than you will ever need. I love to bless you, My child. You need Me so much. You don't know how much you need Me. You are an eternal being; your spirit, soul, and personality are FOREVER, so there's always room for more of My love in you. Receive it more, Sweetness."

I Want to Break Down All the Walls

"Rest in Me, Sweetheart," Father says. "I'm teaching you and filling you with My love. My love for you hasn't diminished, not in the least. I love you so much; My love is FOREVER. I will always love you. I will never, ever leave you or forsake you. Sweetness and Light you are – you bring sweetness and light to dark places."

(I sense God singing this song over me)

I WANT TO BREAK DOWN ALL THE WALLS

Let me fill you with My love/ let Me flood you with My light

Let Me hold you/ Let Me love you, Precious Child

I want to break down all the walls

I want to break through all your pride

So I can love you and fill you with My light

Father Sings Over Me

Then you will shine for Me/ You will shine with My light

If I can hold you and love you and flood you with My light

Oh, I say, Yes, Lord, break down the walls

Break down my pride

So You can fill me and love me and flood me with Your light

Then I will shine for You/ I will shine with Your light

Because You hold me, because You love me

And You flood me with Your light

Yes, Lord, break down all the walls; break down all my pride

Then You will hold me, and You will love me

And You will fill me with Your light

My light is like the light of a thousand stars

Shining brighter than you've ever seen them shine

You shine in just such a way, when you are filled with My light

You are the world's light

And you shine for Me, you shine with My light

Because I hold you and love you, and flood you with My light

Father Sings Over Me

About Pride

"I love you, Princess, and I am healing you," God says. "You are My own precious child. Be strong in Me and in the power of My might. My Holy Spirit indwells you, and I am near you, here with you. I love you, Sweetness. Draw near to Me. I love you so much. My Spirit is within you. Listen. Yes, I led you to the story of King Saul this morning. Saul was deceived by pride. It is important that you not turn to your own way–this is pride. Don't trust in your own ideas and abilities. Trust in <u>Me</u>. Be careful not to go in your own way. You've asked Me to reveal and deal with pride in your life. Whenever you go your own way, this is pride. When you say "later," or when you ignore My still small voice, that's pride. It's important to listen to Me and obey. Listening is the most important thing you do. You have prayed that I show you My ways. I am showing you, and you are coming to know Me. Keep looking to Me, listening to My voice. I want to break down all the walls."

"What walls, Lord?" I ask.

"Pride builds walls so you won't listen or can't hear Me," God says. "Other walls keep you from closeness with Me: guilt and condemnation, unforgiveness, complaining, disobedience and turning your own way."

"Yes, Lord, break down ALL these walls so I can know You more," I respond. "I confess all these walls or sins; please cleanse me. Especially, cleanse me from pride. Break down my pride. I don't want it. Cleanse me from my secret faults, the things I don't know about."

I'm With You *(The Lord gave me this song during a very difficult, frustrating time at work. I felt the Lord singing it over me. I wrote it*

Father Sings Over Me

out on a 3 X 5 card and carried it with me in my pocket at work, and it was and is such a comfort.)

I'M WITH YOU

(Chorus)

I'm with you, I am with you, I'm with you, My child

I'm with you, I am with you, I'm with you, don't be afraid

1) I go before you, I walk beside you
   My arms around you, I carry all your burdens
   I watch behind you as your rear guard

   (Chorus)

2) I'm over you; you're covered with My feathers
   I'm under you to lift you in My arms
   I'm all around you; My love surrounds you

   (Chorus)

3) I'm before you, behind you, beside you to guide you
   I'm over you, I'm under you and I'm in you
   I'm helping you, I'm holding you. I love you.

   (Chorus)

Draw Near (*I woke up very early and God sang this song to me*)

DRAW NEAR TO ME

Draw near to Me, My love

Draw near to Me, My fair one

Father Sings Over Me

I love these times when you draw near

And you can receive My love

Precious, you are precious to Me; I will hold you in My arms

Draw near to Me, My child/ I pour My love out on you

Why did you wait so long to come?

I could have held you in My arms

So draw near

Now, come here

I will help you; I will love you

I will hold you in My arms

Precious, you are precious to Me

I'm helping you, I'm loving you

I'm holding you in My arms

I go back to bed but still get up early enough to meet with God again, and He says, "I called you this morning, Sweetness. It's so good to be with you alone. I'm so glad you've come. I have something to say to you, and you need to be still to hear it. I love it that you got back out of bed and came to Me. I love you. Be a little child so you can see what I have for you. Sit with Me for awhile."

Father Sings Over Me

REST IN ME

Rest in Me alone. Find in Me your peace

Rest in Me alone; you can trust in Me

I love you; you are My child

I love you; you are very My own

You need Me like the flowers need water

You need Me like the birds need their food

Come to Me and find in me your peace

Come to Me and eat and drink your fill

.

Come

Chapter 2

Come

Do Not Be Anxious

"Do not be anxious, fear not," God assures me. "I am with you. Anxiety in your heart weighs you down, but a good word makes you glad. So listen; I have good words for you. I am with you; I never ever leave you or forsake you. I'm helping you and holding you. I love you. Walk in light, Sweetness. You are forgiven. Ask Me when you don't know what to do. I am with you. I love you."

"I have told you not to be anxious about ANYTHING," God says. "Trust Me; bring it all to Me. I love you. You are mine. Take some time today, and don't rush your time with Me. Rest in Me today. I love you. All blessings come from Me. I fill you with My love today. The enemy wants to sift you, to batter your boat with this storm, but don't be afraid; I'm with you. I walk above the trials and storms. I call you to come to Me. Don't look at the problems; look to Me. Invite Me into your boat. Once you know that I am with you, the storm will calm down, and quickly I will bring you to the place where I want you. I am with you, and life is a journey. Don't be afraid. I am with you. I love you. My words are life to you. Listen to My voice saying, 'Take courage. It is I. Do not be afraid.' I have sent you to this place at this time. The storms don't surprise me. Trust Me to bring you through to the other side, and soon you will have solid ground under you again."

Come

Come and Listen

"Words are important," Father says, "especially when they come from your heart. Avoid vain repetition and cliché phrases when you come to Me. You want to praise Me, so praise Me from your heart. Love Me with all your heart, soul, mind and strength. Do you think I can hear you better when you use a lot of words? Speak from the heart; be present with Me, and you will draw closer than you've ever been before. Pay attention like you would with a dear friend, and even closer. Be careful of checking out or zoning out; it wastes time. Focus on Me and on where you are. I love you, and I'll help you."

"I want that, God," I reply. "Father, I want to be closer to You today. You are so good, and Your love is so magnificent and precious. I need You to help me to use my time wisely, to do what You want me to do. I'm like a sheep that goes astray and turns to my own way."

"Yes," God answers, "you so easily go astray, but I laid all that iniquity on My Son. You don't need to stay there, feeling sorry for your sin. Just confess it; tell Me about it and then focus on what I have for you. I'll put you on the right path every time you look to Me and yield to Me. Come to Me. When you're tired, I'll give you rest. Going your own way will not bring rest to your soul. You want to relax and have fun, to escape, but without Me in that, you'll come up empty every time. Learn to look to Me in those moments. You can still relax with Me. You can escape to Me. Run to Me when you're weary. I'll show you what to do. I love you so much."

You Have Come

John 7:37-39: In the last day, that great *day* of the feast, Jesus stood and cried, saying, "If any man thirst, let him come unto Me, and drink. He that believeth on Me, as the scripture hath

Come

said, out of his belly shall flow rivers of living water. (But this He spoke of the Spirit, which they that believe on Him should receive...)

"Yes, Lord, I'm thirsty for You," I respond. "I come to You to drink."

Jesus says, "Drink deeply, Beloved. You were so, so thirsty. You have to drink from Me every day. You can't just go on with only the rhema word I gave you yesterday or the day before. You need My fresh living water today. Come to Me daily, hourly! How often in one day do you need to drink? You may wait four or five hours, but if you wait 10 hours without anything to drink, you will be so thirsty. So it is with your relationship to Me. Recognize your thirst, and come to Me. This is how you will have rivers of living water flowing through you. Keep on coming to Me, Sweetness. I cried out these words, because I want so much for people to hear, to know, and to listen. Whenever you come to Me and truly believe in Me, you will not be thirsty. You cannot be thirsty when the crystal living water is flowing through your inner being. You have come to this river that comes from My throne – waters of life, clear as crystal (Rev 22:1). Drink from My living waters of life, rivers of living water. Don't stay away the way you did yesterday. Let My river flow in and through you. You need this more than natural water and natural food."

He continues, "Let My love take you there. You don't need to get away to another place. You have come. You have come to My heavenly mountain, to the city, and to untold numbers of angels. You are already part of the kingdom of heaven. I am speaking; do not refuse to hear Me. You have come to the spirits of righteousness men made perfect. This is not in the future. You have come. You can be made perfect in this life. My words, My rhema words and My Spirit perfect you. You have come. In coming to Me, you come into

Come

all this. See to it that you do not refuse Me. I am speaking – haven't I told you, I'm always speaking? Come to Me whenever you notice the least bit of thirst for Me. (Heb 12:22-25)

"Be like a tree FIRMLY PLANTED by the streams of My living water," Jesus says. "Don't move away from Me. Meditate on My rhema words day and night. You yield fruit in season, and your leaf will not wither – whatever you do prospers (Psalm 1:2-3). Delight in Me and My rhema words to you and for you."

The City That is My Bride

"I give to you who thirst from the spring of the water of life without cost," Jesus says. "Come, Daughter, I am making all things new. Come to the city that is My Bride; be part of My Bride. You shall see My face, and My name will be on your forehead. You have come to My city. Drink of My river of life–eat of Me."

"Yes, Lord, show me Your face," I say." Open the eyes of my heart so I can see You."

"When you come to Me, you come to My city," He answers. "You are part of My beautiful Bride. Nothing unclean can come in, but you have been washed. You can come in. I light up your life. You have come. Come and drink. You will reign with Me. Be ready as a Bride that says, 'Come' to the rest of the people who have not left their uncleanness, abomination and lying. None of this can enter the city."

"Let the one who is thirsty come." Jesus says. "Let him drink of the water of life freely whenever he wants (Rev 22:17). You are blessed; you may come, for you have washed your robes, and nothing unclean clings to you. Keep your lamp lit, and let My Spirit shine My light on you. I cleanse you from all unrighteousness, and you have

Come

been given a white robe, shining white. My light shines from your eyes. Shine for Me. You've asked Me to break down pride in your life. Delight yourself in Me; fix your eyes on Me, trust Me, and be proud of Me. Boast in this, that you are coming to know Me. Love others with the love I give you. Keep looking to Me; I will show you."

Later in the afternoon: "I love it that you come to Me," God says. "I can give you My rest, Sweetness. Rest in Me. Rest in My love and in My grace. My yoke is EASY, and My burden is <u>light</u>."

You are a Tree Planted by My River

> Ezek. 47:12 And by the river upon the bank thereof, on this side and on that side, shall grow all trees for meat, whose leaf shall not fade, neither shall the fruit thereof be consumed: it shall bring forth new fruit according to his months, because their waters they issued out of the sanctuary: and the fruit thereof shall be for meat, and the leaf thereof for medicine.

"You are a tree planted by My river." God says. "Your fruit is food for others – your leaves are for healing. There are all kinds of trees that grow by My river."

"What kind of tree am I, Lord?" I ask.

I see that I'm like an almond tree, with beautiful white flowers.

"Yes," He answers, "you are like a pretty almond tree. The almond is good food. Your words and actions <u>are</u> <u>life</u> to people. You are planted by My river. Others who come close to My river can eat of your fruit, and your leaves are for healing. Meditate on Me and My words; take delight in Me, and whatever you do will prosper. The almond has oil, anointing oil like you use at the Healing Rooms. The oil is sweet and brings healing. You can use it to anoint your eyes – it

Come

will bring healing. Drink from My pure crystal river; it flows from My throne. Rest in Me. Soak up My light; turn toward the light as a tree does. Lift your hands to Me as a tree lifts its branches. Get this picture – stay planted close to My river – rooted and grounded in good soil. Your leaf will not wither, and you will bear fruit. Eat My words; let them become part of you as a tree pulls nutrients out of the soil. Abide in Me, and let My words abide in you."

No Shame *(I had a troubling dream and was still troubled about it when I went to God in prayer.)*

"Don't worry about that dream," God assures me. "I'm working in your heart and life. Just bring that out-of-sorts, guilty feeling to Me. Let Me wash you whiter than snow. There is NO SHAME with Me. Those who trust in Me will never be put to shame (Psalm 71:1). Wait for Me. You will never be ashamed when you trust and wait on Me (Psalm 25:2-3). Your hope is in Me; I am your refuge. Those who hopefully wait for Me will not be put to shame (Isaiah 49:23). You will not be put to shame or humiliated to all eternity (Isaiah 45:17). Know that you shall not be ashamed (Isaiah 50:7). Fear not, for you will not be put to shame; neither feel humiliated for you will not be disgraced, but you will forget the shame of your youth" (Isaiah 54:4).

"Okay, now listen to Me, look to Me," Father says. "I am speaking. I cover your shame. I clothe you with My righteousness. Give it to Me. Confess it to Me. I will clothe you in a white robe – brilliant, beautiful white like sparkling diamonds that reflect all colors like a shimmering rainbow. Heavenly white is different from earthly white and much better. I wash you whiter than snow. There will be those who disapprove of you, but if you wait on Me and trust in Me, you will never be ashamed."

Come

Heavenly White

(At Redeeming Love Church, evening of "His Presence")

"Come up here, right here to Me," God says. "Come to Me and drink; you're so thirsty. Drink of the pure crystal stream of living water, SPARKLING and pure. Come to Me and drink; be refreshed in My river, and your thirst will be quenched. Float in My river, and the living crystal water will wash you whiter than snow. Beautiful, sparkling white – iridescent white with hints of every color of the rainbow and colors you have never seen, heavenly white, dazzling like diamonds. The white robe I give you is white like this – heavenly white. The river that washes you comes from My throne; you can come right to the source that bubbles up to eternal life. Eternal life is knowing Me."

**In my mind's eye, I can see God's river; the water is so clear and pure. I imagine myself drinking from God's river of life, bathing in the river and coming out with a sparkling white robe, whiter than any white on earth.

(Note: I shared this word with the people at the "His Presence" service, and I could imagine all the people there dressed in heavenly white robes, like God described. Heaven is so wonderful, and in the Spirit, we are already there!)

Crystal Waters

"Focus on Me and on My river," Father says. "My pure, living, crystal waters cleanse you. Let My river flow deeper in you; let it flow more. Yes, look at the word I gave you on Saturday night *(see "No Shame")*. Come up to My throne where the river begins. Let my Spirit, My river of living water carry you from here at My throne. Precious One, My

Come

river is filled with love and light. Yes, like the rivers you saw in *Uruapan*, only brighter, with more light. If the river carries you, you are carried by My love. Float in My crystal, sparkling bright river. I'm with you. I'm all around you. I carry you. Rest in Me. I love you. You are so precious to Me. You are My princess, and everything I have is yours."

(Note on Uruapan: John and I had visited a water paradise park in Uruapan, Michoacán, Mexico, with some missionary friends. The water was so crystal clear; it reflected the sunlight in such a way in the rapids and falls that it looked like there were lights under the water. Pictures of this are on the front and back covers of this book. It was very beautiful and amazing.)

Be a Little Child

"I'm with you," God says. "You are Mine and I am yours. I love you, Sweetness. I'm holding you and helping you. I'm with you. I give you joy in knowing Me."

** I'm with Jesus walking through a beautiful field of wild flowers. I'm a little girl going on a walk with Him, noticing the flowers, trees and butterflies; the clear blue sky and the sunshine. "Jesus, what do You say to me?" I ask.

Jesus takes me down to the brook and show me how I can drink from the cool, clear water. I can sit on the bank and dangle my feet in the water – so refreshing!

"Your time with Me is like this," Jesus replies, "a time of rest and reflection, alone with Me. You need to be like a little child and just be with Me. As I lead you, you will see what I want you to see. Soak up the sunshine of My love and joy. Enjoy the atmosphere of Heaven.

Come

Come with Me, and I will show you things as naturally as going for a walk through a field and coming upon a brook.

"Focus on Me," Jesus says. "I am the One who cleanses you. My pure, crystal, sparkling river of life flows from My throne, and you can come to Me and drink. Drink deeply, Beloved. Be refreshed. The sun is shining, the grass is green and there are flowers and birds. Colors you have never seen before. Sit on the bank of My river and dangle your feet in the life-giving stream."

**I see Jesus wading in the river, and He splashes me. There is great joy and playfulness. "Yes," He says, "rest here and delight in Me, Beloved. I'm with you, sharing this moment."

You Have a Crown

"Keep seeking the things above, where I am seated at the right hand of My Father," Jesus says. "Set your mind on the things above, not on the things that are on the earth, for you have died and your life is hidden with Me in God. Yes, seek the river coming from My throne – the water of life – the Holy Spirit. Seek the tree of life – eat of the tree of life which is in the PARADISE of God (Rev 2:7). Eat of the hidden manna – all you need is in Me (Rev 2:17). I give you a white stone – you are free in Me, and all My promises are 'YES' for you. I write your name on the stone, 'Sweetness', but also a new name that you will know right away when I call you by it. I give you authority over nations if you overcome and keep My deeds until the end, and I will give you the morning star (Rev 2:26-28). Be an overcomer – overcome the feelings of aimlessness and inadequacy. You are a princess in My house. You have a crown."

**I see the crown, gold and silver with leaves of silver on a gold base – very shiny with blue topaz stones and aquamarine and sapphires

Come

and diamonds, a heavenly crown. "I want it," I say to Jesus. "You tell me to seek those things above, to set my mind on those things."

"Yes," Jesus answers, "I have a crown for you (Rev. 2:10). You are a princess. Hold your head up. You will walk with Me in white, heavenly white, dazzling with every color of the rainbow, sparkling like diamonds (Rev 3:4-5). I will make you a pillar in My temple – you can stay in My presence, and not go out from My presence anymore, but on you will be the name of My Father, the name of the city of God, the new Jerusalem, and My new name. All this will be written on you. My love for you can be written all over your face. NO MORE shame (Rev 3:12). Sit here with Me on My throne – yes, this is here and NOW. I speak from heaven – come up here! Overcome, and you are seated with Me. You walk with Me. You are <u>Mine</u>" (Rev 3:21).

"Seek these things," He encourages me, "the things which are above. Do not refuse Me; I am speaking to you (Heb 12:25). Listen – you have come to Mount Zion and to My heavenly city and to countless angels. Be <u>heavenly minded</u>. You are enrolled in heaven and there is a place for you here (Heb 12:22-23). Drink from My heavenly river. Walk with Me on the streets of gold, clothed in white."

You Have Come to My Throne

"My throne is awesome in appearance, as are the cherubim who attend Me," God says. "Were you to see Me, you would also fall down as dead (Rev. 1:17, 4:2-8). You would need My words and My touch to stand before Me. But when the Spirit entered Ezekiel, he could stand before Me (Ezek. 1:28-2:2). I recorded this for your benefit, so you can see with your mind's eye. Yes, I am awesome, but remember that I love you. In the Spirit you have come to My throne and to the Lamb. In My presence the elders cast their crowns; in the presence of My Son, they fall down and worship. They shout

Come

'Worthy' – all angels worship Me and My Son with a loud voice along with every creature on earth and under the earth. Fix your eyes on Jesus. Run the race I have for you, and don't quit (Heb. 12:1-2). You have come to My throne, to My angels – it is revealed and written. I am speaking what was written to you. It is all yours. My Spirit shows you that it belongs to you. The experience of John and Ezekiel is yours as you read of it and see it in your mind's eye. See it. Look at Me. Look to Me. Heaven is yours; it is your destiny and your inheritance – heaven and the city and the mountain of God."

Take Another Drink

"You are so thirsty," Father says. "Come to Me and drink. Drink in the life giving flow of My words within you. I Am the life. Take another drink from My river, Sweetness. The waters are pure as crystal, sparkling clear and refreshingly sweet. Come to the waters. Drink of the waters of life freely. I love you. My love for you is like cool, sweet water; refreshing and pure. Drink deeply, beloved. Let My love fill you like cool water on a hot day. Let Me satisfy your thirsty soul. I love you so much. Rest in Me, and receive from Me now."

Chapter 3

Walk With Me

Among the Trees *(Afternoon in early spring in St Paul, Minnesota)*

I'm on a long walk and hear the Lord saying, "Walk with Me in the trees." I feel a strange drawing or attraction to the trees near Lake Phalen along Johnson Parkway. I feel like Jesus is walking in those trees and I need to walk with Him. I keep hearing Him say, "Walk with Me among the trees." As I walk there, I see community among the trees. Several of them stand in a circle. They have a faithful, steadfast steadiness of giving space to one another. I look up and see that although the branches come close to each other, they don't touch; the branches are overlapping but not pushing each other out.

As I look, I see an eagle flying above the trees and soaring higher and higher. I watch the eagle for some time, until it soars so high that I can no longer see it with my naked eye. Then God says, "As you wait on Me you are like that eagle, soaring on the wind. You can walk with Me and wait on Me even though there is busy hustle and bustle of cars and people rushing all around you. I am pleased that you take time to walk and talk with Me. I gave you vision at a young age; you look at things differently from others, seeing tiny details. You notice how the sun shines bright on the new growth on the trees and how there are new yellow branches on the trees by the lake. You appreciate the varying shades of beautiful blue in the sky and the pinkish grey of the clouds."

Walk With Me

Walk the Ancient Paths

"When you see something in the Spirit," God explains, "like yesterday with the trees, come close to look, and I will speak to you and show you more. I have more to tell you about the trees. The trees are planted, steady and faithful. They represent believers, pillars in the church, and teachers. Walk the ancient paths with Me. Study the writings of those gone by like St. Francis of Assisi. Ask [your friend who reads a lot] what he would recommend. Walk with Me among the trees. I am with you. I will teach you. Yes, you see yourself walking among the trees further down and sitting there this summer. Do this, and I will speak to you. Today, I am with you. I will help you. I give you wisdom and grace. I'm going with you to the new house. Look to Me today. Ask Me, and I will show you what to do. I love you, and I will help you. Do the things you see yourself doing."

(Note: We had just bought a house, and I was going there to clean and get things ready to move.)

Pure Crystal Water

"Drink of My living water," God says. "Wade in — come on in; the water is fine. Float in the river of My Spirit and be refreshed by My pure crystal water. Let Me wash away all the cares. Float in My river and be carried."

Shine for Me

"No shame," Father says. "Trust in Me, and you shall NEVER be put to shame. No shame; I gave My Son to take your shame and remove your guilt. He was Himself your guilt offering (Isaiah 53:10). In the flesh, in your own strength you cannot please Me, but you are not in the flesh, but in the Spirit; My Spirit indwells you. Even if parts of

Walk With Me

your body are dead because of sin, My Spirit indwells you and shall give LIFE to your body (Rom 8:8-11). It's all because of what I have done for you, because I love you. I don't see you as you were; I see you as you are and even more, I see what you will become. You are My child, My very own, a princess in My house, and I am your Daddy. You are washed in the blood – sanctified, set apart for Me. You wear a white robe of My righteousness. You shine for Me, Precious, brilliant and beautiful. Stand before Me and bask in My radiance, and you will reflect My glory."

**Jesus stands before me and puts His hands on my shoulders. "I love you," He says. "My love is all that matters. It is enough and more than enough for you. I clothe you with My righteousness. I do not condemn you – I justify you because you trust in Me. You reflect My glory. You are clothed in heavenly white with blue tones; sky blue and bright. You shine for Me. You like blue, because it's the color of heaven. The sky reflects the light of the sun. You reflect My light and My glory. Your blue eyes shine with a light that comes from the heavenly kingdom within. Being in My presence is so important. Wait on Me, and you will have renewed strength."

Like an Eagle

"Wait on Me, and you will fly," God says. "Mount up on wings like an eagle. You will soar and ride on the wind of My Spirit. You will fly higher than you ever thought possible. You will be able to see from a new perspective. This is the most important thing you do – take time waiting on Me, and you will fly high above all your circumstances. You will renew your strength, and you will REST on the wind of My Spirit. Come fly with Me."

Walk With Me

Fly With Me

"Lord, how important is it to use the eyes of my heart?" I ask. "How have I been using them, and how do You want me to use them?"

God answers, "You have been learning to use the eyes of your heart. Continue to learn, but you don't need to hurry. One day at a time. You can start with the images you've already seen: the trees, the eagle, the river, the heavenly city, and the white garments. Look closer at any one of these, and I will show you MORE."

**I think about and visualize the eagle, and God says, "The eagle can go high and far without expending any extra energy. If you wait on Me, you will gain new strength — you mount up on wings like an eagle. You gain My strength. Ride on the wind of My Spirit — fly with Me. Today. stop, look and listen; then do what you see or hear next."

Walk With Me by My River

"My river is strong," God says. "There are places where it rushes and falls, and others where it's peaceful and still, because it widens into a lake. Walk with Me by My river; walk in the Spirit. Listen to Me, and stay by Me. Be yoked together with Me today. My yoke is EASY. My burden is light. My love for you is greater, higher, wider, and deeper than you can possibly imagine. I am able to do SO MUCH MORE than you can ask or think (Eph 3:18-20). My love surpasses all knowledge, but you can know it. I grant to you a spirit of wisdom and revelation in the knowledge of Me. The eyes of your heart are being ENLIGHTENED, so you can know the hope of your calling. I want you to know the riches of the glory of My inheritance in the saints... the city, the river, My throne, the light of My presence. I want you to know My great power; the surpassing greatness of My power toward you and all who believe" (Eph 1:17-19).

Walk With Me

A Plan and a Destiny

"I want to hear from You!" I plead with God. "I want to see You! This is the cry of my heart, Father. Open the eyes of my heart, open my ears to listen. Let me hear Your voice and see Your face, or at least, see what You want me to see, Father."

"I AM like no other," Father answers. "There is nothing, no one who can touch you the way I can. I formed you in the womb. I made you. I am the maker of ALL things. I planted you in this earth like the tree in your yard. I decided where you would be born. The previous owner who planted that tree in your yard planned where to plant it, but I had all wisdom, knowledge and foresight when I formed you. I had a plan and a destiny for you. Even as I keep the stars and planets on the course I have chosen for them, even so I can keep you on the path I have chosen for you. You are more precious to Me than many stars. My Holy Spirit is within you. You are made in My image, and you have come into My light. You shine for Me. Walk in My light. Shine with My light. I, the Lord, am the Maker of all things, stretching out the heavens by Myself and spreading out the earth all alone (Isaiah 44:24). I have a plan for you for today. Look to Me every step of the way, and I will lead and guide you."

Let My Spirit Fill You More

"I'm with you. My Spirit fills you," God says.

"Could You fill me more, Holy Spirit?" I ask.

"Yes. Yes. Yes," He answers. "Nothing I would rather do. Wait on Me and I will fill you. Ask Me."

"Fill me, fill my house, Lord," I plead. "Holy Spirit come. Come more. I'm desperate for You, for more of You."

Walk With Me

"Okay, you've asked; now wait on Me," He answers. "Can you just be still and wait for 10 minutes? I am for you. I'm on your side. Wait for Me; it will be worth it. I wrap My love around you like a warm blanket. I'm holding you and loving you, Precious One. I breathe on you, and I fill you more. There is room in your spirit for more of Me, because your spirit is ETERNAL. Your soul is the part of you that can change, renew, heal, and form into what I want you to be. Your soul will be with Me for eternity as well... Your spirit and soul are with Me. Your spirit is joined to My Spirit, and so you are in HEAVEN in the Spirit. My Spirit brings comfort and rest, but also joy and excitement and electricity and awe and wonder. Let My Spirit fill you MORE, and you will be amazed and ASTOUNDED. You see, you don't realize how much you need Me; you need Me to fill you MORE."

"Yes, Holy Spirit," I answer. "Fill me more!"

"That's good," Holy Spirit encourages me. "Now your heart is crying out for it, for Me to fill you MORE. Yes, keep asking for more of Me throughout the day today. You have been doing so much in your own strength. You need My anointing for every task – for cleaning, unpacking, for cooking. I anoint you now. Look to Me, and I will anoint you for every task today. Keep asking Me to fill you MORE, and I will do just that. I breathe on you. I will lead you today."

Song: "Draw Me" (*It's early spring in Minnesota. On my walk by Lake Phalen, I sing this song to Jesus.*)

DRAW ME

Draw me, and I will run after You

Tug on my hand, pull at my heart

I will run after You. Draw me

Walk With Me

Jesus, I don't want to stay the way I was

Draw me closer together with You. Draw me

Let me hold Your hand, and we can walk together

It's the cry of my heart to be closer to You

"Yes, I will draw you closer than you've ever been before," Jesus responds. "Come with Me, My love, My fair one. I'll help you with all you have to do. Ask Me. Take My yoke; it's easy. I will help you with every task. I will give you wisdom. Set your mind on Me and what I'm doing. Do the things you see Me doing. Take My yoke; learn from Me. I am meek and humble of heart. I humbled Myself to come to you. I am still meek and humble. I love to serve you and teach you. I care about you so much. I love you so much. I am yours. I created all this – the way light reflects off the soft waves, the perpetual motion of the waves and the way the waves push the rocks up onto the shore. Peace. This is a peaceful place for you. I prepared it for you. Don't be anxious; I am with you. I will help you with everything. I take you to where you have never been before. These are times and seasons, and this is a new day. There are signs of new life all around you. Bushes and trees are budding."

Chapter 4

A Little Child With Jesus

Just Hold My Hand

**I'm a little child with blond hair, about four or five years old, and I am wearing a blue shirt and darker blue pants. I'm holding Jesus' hand and walking with Him. The grass is green; the sun is shining. Long, tall grass sways in the wind, and yellow and pink butterflies flutter around the wildflowers.

"Just hold My hand, Sweetness, and be with Me," Jesus says. "I will take you where you need to go. Rest in Me." We run and skip through the flowers together.

Jesus brings me to the shore of a little lake; there are trees around it. We wade into the water. "Don't worry about getting your pants wet. It's warm, and they will dry," Jesus assures me. "Give Me your heart, Little One, Baby Girl."

After we're done wading, I sit on Jesus' lap, and He dries my feet with His white homespun robe. He brushes the sand off my little toes. We walk barefoot in the soft grass. I stoop down to look at a tiny yellow flower in the short grass. He stoops down and looks at the flower, too, and tenderly touches my hair.

"Be a child with Me," Jesus says. "Don't try so hard to know everything at once. Rest in Me, Sweetness. Just hold My hand. Let Me take care of you. I'm holding your hand and watching over you."

A Little Child with Jesus

Humble Yourself like a Child

**I'm with Jesus, looking at that little flower. The sun is shining on my hair, and Jesus touches it. He squats down to see the flower. "Be a little child with Me, Patty. This is the most important thing you need to know right now: become like a child. Humble yourself as a little child, and you will be greatest in the kingdom of Heaven. Hold My hand; walk with Me as a little child. Keep your sense of wonder. My kingdom belongs to those who are child-like in their trust and belief in Me. I lay My hands on you. I take you in My arms and bless you (Mark 10:13-16, Matt. 18:1-6 & 10). The kingdom of God belongs to those who are child-like in their belief and trust in Me. Humble yourself like a child. Receive the kingdom of God like a child (Luke 18:15-17). Like a baby, long for the pure milk of the word."

Jesus picks me up and holds me up high. He swings me around in the air like I'm flying; it makes me giggle. He carries me as He walks, smiling. His right arm is around me, and I'm so secure and happy.

Father and the Holy Spirit

"Father, You are like this, too," I realize. "You are like Jesus."

"I am everything that Jesus is and MORE," Father responds. "I love to be with you. I love to bless My children. My blessing is on you today, and I'm touching you."

(Later —walking under the trees) "Be still and know that I am God," He says. "I'm here; I am with you."

**I see myself waiting with a peaceful look of anticipation on my face. The Holy Spirit comes in a sparkly cloud in front of my face, and I breathe Him in. "I make all things new for you," He says.

A Little Child with Jesus

Now Father comes to me. I can't see Him, but I know He wraps me in His arms. "Oh, Sweetness," He says, "wait on Me, and you will renew your strength. Like an eagle, you soar on the wind effortlessly. Take time with Me. The time you spend with Me is the MOST important thing. Precious One, it's okay that you don't hear or see a lot. What I have shown you today is enough. My love for you is greater than you can possibly imagine. I am with you."

You Shine For Me/ Liquid Love

"I want to see improvement in my relationships at work," I say. "I want to pray for my co-workers." *(I pray for each one by name…)*

"You are a light to these people," God replies. "You shine for Me among them. I have sent you to them. I sent you, and I have a plan for each one for their lives. Ask Me, and I'll give you words for them. Think about Heaven – set your mind on My river, My throne, the new Jerusalem, the new earth. I will make PEACE your administrators, and RIGHTEOUSNESS your overseers (Isaiah 60:17). You will have Me, the Lord, for your everlasting light; I will be your GLORY" (Isaiah 60:19-20).

"Step into the part of this that I have already given to you," He continues. "I am light, and in Me is <u>NO</u> darkness at all. I light up your life from the inside. I am your light. Be filled with My light, and you will shine for Me. Believe in Me, and out of your innermost being will flow RIVERS of living water. I give you My Spirit – I baptize you in My Spirit."

**There's a floating liquid heart like a water-filled red heart balloon, only it floats. Jesus is sending it as liquid love. It hits me and splats all over me, and now I love everyone. I have red Kool-Aid-like stains all over me, but they're heart shaped. Some of the liquid love soaks

33

A Little Child with Jesus

right into me. I have a heart on my arm, and as I hug someone, the heart comes out of me and splashes onto them. I can launch a liquid love heart just as Jesus did! I can direct it at a person, and the same will happen to them.

"I want to fill you with My love like that," God says. "Be like a little child, and receive it and give it."

Living Water

**I'm a little child, and Jesus and I are swimming in the little lake. He disappears under the water for a minute, so I don't know where He is. Then He pops up next to me with a big grin on His face. He puts me on His back, and I grab onto His robe and ride on His back as He swims under water again very fast. We come to the place where a small stream flows into the little lake, and we wade up the stream, walking on the rocks, hand in hand. We're exploring in the trees. There are trees and woods. The stream is about four feet wide and a few inches deep, and the water runs pretty fast. We sit down to rest on the side, on a little grassy bank, our feet still in the water. The water is crystal clear. "You can drink this water – it comes from My throne – drink". He reaches down and cups His hand and brings the water to my mouth. I drink, and He says, "Let the living water of My Spirit flow through you today."

Clothed in My Spirit

"Wait on Me for 10 more minutes," God says, "then get ready for your day. Look to Me. I want to speak to your heart. You are so precious to Me, My little girl. You are a precious jewel. I put a crown on your head with silver and gold and blue topaz, sapphires and diamonds. You are wearing a sky blue royal robe. You are part of the kingdom of heaven, a princess in My kingdom. You are clothed with

A Little Child with Jesus

heaven – white mink (represents the clouds) trims your satin gown, and you have blue satin slippers. Stay close to Me, and others will be able to see how precious you are. I take you by the hand. I lead you beside the peaceful stream. You are clothed in My Spirit – your gown represents the river – clear blue and sparkling – beautiful and holy."

Manna

**I'm sitting next to Jesus by the stream, drinking the water. Our feet are in the water, and He says, "Drink more, Patty. Let My Spirit fill you. Be a child. Eat what I give you. I am the Bread of Life." Jesus turns and points to the grassy bank behind Him. There is manna scattered in the grass. We gather some manna, and I eat it. "Eat My words," He says. "My words are spirit and life to you" (John 6:63).

Be That Baby Girl

"Sweetness and Light, I send you as light today. Shine for Me," God says. "I fill you with My light and love. You are My very own precious child. Be the child you are. Have you noticed how much children smile? A baby's smile can light up a whole room full of grumpy people. Be that baby girl to people; shine for Me. Look people in the eyes and smile. Sing for them. Keep the joy; keep My joy in your heart."

See How Much I Love You

**I'm a little girl standing by the stream, holding Jesus' hand. Jesus stoops down and strokes my hair with one hand, cups my chin in the other and says, "Look at Me, Sweetness. See how much I love you." There is great love and tenderness in His eyes and in His smile. "I'm taking care of you. I love you so much. My love makes you a princess. Remember that I'm always with you, Sweetness. My arm is around

A Little Child with Jesus

you while you are at work. I'm helping you. Ask Me whenever you don't know what to do, I'm right with you. I will strengthen you and help you. You are My child. I love you, and My Father loves you. Give all your worries and cares to Me."

Come as a Child

"I'm with you," He says. "Come to Me as a little child today. I love you. You are so precious to Me, My little Princess, My little Sunshine, Sweetness and Light. I love you so much. Let Me fill you with My love."

**Jesus picks me up. I'm a little girl, and He holds me on His lap, there under the trees. He strokes my hair affectionately. He smiles at me, a big smile, full of love and affection for me. I smile back at Him. He bounces me on His knee, and I laugh. He laughs with me and hugs me – there is such love in His hugs. "Receive My love," He says. "Take it, and be filled with it. Be wrapped in My love today like a big strong hug!"

Liquid Love

"Listen to My words," Father says. "Let My words of love and wisdom fill your heart. I love you with an everlasting love. I've always loved you and always will. Before you were born, I saw you and loved you. You are so very precious to Me. My love can fill you – let Me fill you now. Rest in My love. Rest – let My peace fill you. My love wraps itself around you. I have My arms around you. I fill you with love so it can spill over on to others."

** I'm a little girl with Jesus. He holds me in His arms and fills me with His love. Then He sends me off to play with the other children. The love that's in me radiates from me like red cartoon hearts, only

A Little Child with Jesus

liquid. It splashes out of me, and the hearts float all around me. I go to play with the others, and my love splashes on them, and they smile with love for me in return.

One little girl stands off to the side alone. She looks so sad and left out. I go to her, and my love splashes on her but kind of splashes off again, because she can't receive it. So I take her by the hand and bring her to Jesus. He crouches down, arms open for her to come, but she hesitates. I put my arm around her shoulders and walk with her over to Jesus. We both walk into Jesus' arms, and He puts us both on His lap. Now His liquid love is filling us both. She cries into His chest. He gently wipes the tears from her face, and as He touches her face, peace comes on it. Then she smiles, and she is much prettier. The change in her face shows that she has received Jesus' love.

(This vision touches me deeply, and I know that Jesus wants me to share His love with others. He wants to use me to bring others to Him.)

You Need My Love More Than Anything

**I'm coming to Jesus as a little girl again. He holds me again, because I need it. "You need My love more than anything. I want you to be continually filled with it. I love you. My love is what you need – perfect love casts out all fear. My love is all you need to give you security. "

Chapter 5

I'm Taking Care of You

I Love You More

It's such a beautiful, perfect day in mid-May in Minnesota. I'm sitting out in the back yard under the flowering apple trees. Amazing, how quickly everything has blossomed out and grown! "Thank you, Father!" I exclaim. "It's so beautiful!"

"Sweetness," God says, "you are beautiful, and I love you. I love you more than all these things. You are so precious to Me. I want to touch your heart and fill you with My love."

Sweetness and Light

Isaiah 55:11: "You are a princess in My Father's house," Jesus says. "Walk in assurance of your authority. You are seated with Me in heavenly places. Let My love fill you. Drink of My river of life – My Spirit fills you more."

"Sweetness and Light, I call your name," God says. "You have cried out to Me, for more of Me – there's nothing I'd rather do. I want to fill you more, Princess. I draw you, and you can run after Me. I love you. Be a little child with Me – be more and more like a child."

Cast Your Burdens on Me

"Are you thirsty?" Jesus asks. "Come to Me and drink. I'll fill you, and rivers of living water will flow from you. Drink Beloved; drink of My

I'm Taking Care of You

Spirit of love. Believe Me; believe in Me, and you will do greater works than I did. Yes, you need to believe in Me MORE. My Spirit is in you, and you are never alone. Believe that your hands are My hands. You are part of My body. My Spirit helps you and teaches you."

"Lord," I say, "my neck and back feel better today after John prayed for me, but I still have pain in the neck. Why am I not completely healed?"

"Cast all your burdens on Me," He answers. "You forget that I'm right here all the time, ready to help you and carry all your burdens. Sweetness, give it all to Me. Have a thankful heart. Read Phil 4:8 and do what it says; think on good things."

"Before I go, is there something You want me to see?"

Brick Vision *(This vision I have shared with many people, and it may apply to you as well.)*

** I have a heavy backpack full of bricks on my back. Each one has a name of something I'm concerned about on it. Jesus helps me take off the backpack, and we look at each brick: house, mess, job, and furniture, Mary Jo, David and Peter, East Side Healing Rooms...

With each one, He asks me, "Will you let Me take care of this for you?" When I hand the brick to Him, He tenderly holds it and promises, "I'll take care of this for you." Then He neatly piles the bricks into a little wall, and I'm surprised that there are about 15 bricks I was carrying!

"Make sure you bring me all your cares; I care for you," Jesus says. When the backpack is empty, He asks me, "Can you give Me that, too?" I give it to Him and He puts the backpack behind the little wall.

I'm Taking Care of You

** The next day I'm back in the same vision, and Jesus is sitting on that little wall of bricks. He's sitting on my problems! "Tell Me what's on your heart. Talk to Me. I love you so much. I know all that you need, and I supply all your needs. I'm with you. I'll help you."

Then He looks me in the eyes and says, "You were not meant to carry any burdens."

Rest for Your Soul

"I'm with you to help you today," Jesus assures me. "You are mine, Sweetness. You know that I love you. I love you more than you know. Let My love fill you until you overflow. I'm taking care of you. Take My yoke upon you today. You will find rest for your soul. Today, as you work, your soul will find rest in Me. My yoke is EASY, and My burden is light (Matt. 11:28-30). I satisfy the weary ones and refresh everyone who languishes (Jer. 31:25). Are you thirsty? Come to Me and drink (John 7:37). Learn from Me, and do as I do; serve (John 13:15). Be renewed in the Spirit of your mind, and put on the new self (Eph. 4:23-24). Have the same attitude I have; empty yourself (Phil. 2:5,7). Follow in My steps (I Pet. 2:21). Abide in Me, and you will walk in the way I walked (I John 2:6). My commands are not burdensome (I John 5:3). Walk in the good way, and you will find REST for your soul (Jer. 6:16). I am with you every step of the way!"

Blue Represents Heaven

"Okay now, be still and listen to Me," God says. "Focus on Me, look to Me. I'm here with you. I forgive you for getting distracted. Give today to Me. I love you more than you can ever imagine. Be still a few more minutes. Princess, your favorite color is blue, and blue represents heaven. I clothe you in a beautiful blue dress and over that a royal blue robe. Can you see it? Walk with Me, Princess. Walk

I'm Taking Care of You

with Me in heavenly gardens. My arm is around you, and I hold your right hand in Mine. As we walk, My strength goes into you. I am leading and guiding you in all that you do. I'm with you as you go through your day. Remember that you are a princess with Me and that I'm with you today."

My Words are Life to You

"Abraham believed Me that I am good," Father says. "He believed in My love for him, and so he offered up Isaac at My command, at My word. His faith was shown by his works (James 2:21-23). Believe Me and every rhema word that comes from My Spirit to you. My words are LIFE to you and health to ALL your whole body. My words are important for you spiritual, mental, and physical health (Prov. 4:22). Live by My every word that proceeds from My mouth. Hang on to My words, and you will be happy and blessed, and you will have PEACE (Prov. 3:17-18).

"Your path is like the light of dawn that shines brighter and brighter until the full day when you are with Me. Before dawn, there are only shades of grey, and you cannot see clearly. One day you will see many things you never saw before, but even in this life, your path shines brighter and brighter (Prov. 4:18). Listen.... I am always speaking, so listen to My words. My words give life to you. Fix the eyes of your heart on Me. Yes, see how much I love you; that's what you need to know most. Be the little girl that you are, and don't try to know too much. Be comforted by My love. Let My love fill you, Sweetness. Let My love touch your heart and fill you with My joy.

"Sit here on My lap, and now let Me carry you. You try to carry burdens, but you were never meant to carry them. Give me all those burdens, all those bricks. I'll take care of them for you. David and his future, Peter and his future, your job, East Side Healing Rooms and

I'm Taking Care of You

the team, eating and what you should eat, supplements, your knees, hips, back and neck – your whole body. Don't be anxious about these people or things. I'll take care of them: your house, your Mom and Dad and even your son's pet rabbit. Yes, there are things for you to do, but they are meant to be a <u>joy</u> and not a burden. Let My <u>Joy</u> fill you. Knowing that I love you is the most important thing. You are so VERY PRECIOUS to Me. Rejoice in that. Anxiety in your heart weighs you down and makes you tired, but a good word makes you <u>GLAD</u>. This is your good word – I love you; I fill you with My love and joy. You are precious to Me, and I carry ALL your burdens if you give them to Me. Cast all your burdens on Me, for I care for you. You are My little child, and I love to take care of you; it gives Me joy. Rest in Me today, and let Me lead you. You've been working for several days – rest today."

Living Stones Vision

Living Stones Vision

Chapter 6

Living Stones Vision

(Note: This vision starts here and continues over several days, and I continue to get more revelation even more than a year later.)

With Jesus by the Stream

**I'm sitting with Jesus on the edge of the stream. We have our feet in the water. We've just taken a drink from the stream. I'm a little girl. Jesus smiles at me with such love in His eyes. He says, "Take another drink, and now look around you."

The sun is shining. There are tall, beautiful trees; their leaves sparkle in the warm breeze and blue sky. I climb onto Jesus' lap and lean my head back on His chest. He puts His arms around Me. "Rest in Me, Sweetness. Be a little child. I give you REST. I love you, Baby Girl." We get up and pick some flowers. Jesus gives me a clay vase to put them in with water from the stream. I set them on the flat rocks near the bank but still in the stream.

Beautiful Stones

**I'm with Jesus by the stream. I've just placed the flowers in the clay jar on the rocks in the stream. "You are beautiful like the flowers in the clay jar," Jesus tells me. "You are My treasure in an earthen vessel. You are soft and delicate, more beautiful than any flowers. I make you to grow and bloom for Me. As a tight little peony bud opens up and becomes a large beautiful bloom, bursting with color

43

Living Stones Vision

and fragrance that praises Me — so are you, as you open up to Me. Remember to be like a little child. You are My child, My very own. The time you spend with Me is NEVER wasted. Sweetness, Precious Flower, just be with Me. I will help you; I will show you My ways. I love you <u>so</u> <u>much</u>. I'm with you today. Stay close to Me."

I notice beautiful stones in the stream. I start picking them up; blue stones, pink shiny stones, stones of all different pastel colors. I pick them up and put them on the rock near the flowers. *(I think about and read I Pet. 2:4-5: "You also as living stones are being built up as a spiritual house.")*

"These stones have been worn smooth and polished in My living water," Jesus tells me. "So they are living stones. Take time soaking in My river, and you will be a living stone suitable for My spiritual house, connected to Me as the precious cornerstone."

Jesus and I will build a little house with the stones. I start to line stones up for the start of the walls. I line them up in four rows, forming the shape of a square. Jesus brings a stone, and I know it's the cornerstone, but this cornerstone is a lot bigger and an odd shape. By my own understanding, the stone is not one I would choose for the little house, but Jesus brings it and places it next to my pile of stones. The stone is "a living stone which has been rejected by men, but is choice and precious in the sight of God" (I Pet 2:4). The stone is white with cracks and a very uneven angular shape. Looking at it, I wonder how it will work. "The stone which the builders rejected, this became the very cornerstone" (I Pet 2:7). I really want to know how the stone fits with the other. It's so much bigger, and it has such a different shape. Jesus doesn't show me today...

Living Stones Vision

My Living Stone

**I'm in the stream again with Jesus, by the rock with the flowers and the stones we collected. Jesus says, "Come with me now. We can come back later and finish the house." We have collected quite a pile of stones along with the big cornerstone. I pick up a pretty blue one from the pile. It's a light, translucent, aqua blue.

"That one is like you," Jesus says. "It matches your outfit, and it will go in your crown someday. You can take it with you." I hold the stone in my little right hand, and Jesus takes my left, and we wade in the stream – up stream. We come to a place where there is a tree fallen across the stream. Jesus picks me up and carries me over it. "I'm with you to help you," He says. "I'm taking care of you." I look at the stone in my hand. It seems to have a light from within. "Yes, it's a living stone, and it has its own light," Jesus says. "My light is within you, and your eyes shine with My love. Sweetness and Light you are. I love to spend time with you. Take time to be alone with Me. Get in the stream of My Spirit, My living waters. Drink from the stream, let the waters wash over you."

First, I put the stone in my pocket, then we sit down in the stream, and the water rushes over our legs. I laugh and play in the water. Jesus cups His hand and gives me a drink. The water is so sweet and refreshing, and I can feel it bring joy to my insides. The sound of the rushing water is like music. "My words are water to your soul – soothing and healing. Let My loving words fill you. Take another drink, Sweetness. Let My JOY fill you. Rejoice in Me, just a few more minutes..."

(I sing) Behold, God is my Salvation. I will trust and not be afraid, for the Lord, my God, is my strength and my song. He also has become my salvation. Therefore, with joy will you draw water up from the

Living Stones Vision

wells of your salvation. And in that day will you say, "Praise the Lord," and make mention that His name is exalted (Isaiah 12:2-4).

Reflections of Glory!

I'm walking by Lake Phalen in Minnesota. It's a beautiful day. It rained last night, and the rain drops in the grass reflect the morning sun. I keep looking at them and notice they sparkle like diamonds – reflecting blue, green and yellow. I find one that reflects red, then as I move from side to side looking at it from different angles, it acts as a perfect little prism, and I can see all the colors of the rainbow; red, orange, yellow, green, blue, indigo, violet. Reflections of Glory!!! Praise You, God!

(Next day) "My loving kindness is new every morning," God says. "I have great things for you today. You are like that rain drop you looked at yesterday, reflecting My Glory."

Think About the Things You Have Seen

I'm thinking about the cornerstone and the living stones, trying to figure out how they fit together.

"You don't need to know how everything works," God explains. "That's My job. I'm with you, Precious One. I love you so much. You are so special to Me. You can wait for Me to reveal things to you. Think about the things you have seen, the things revealed belong to you. You are a little child. You are My precious baby girl. Sweetness, I love you. I have things to show you, like the raindrop the other day *(see Reflections of Glory)*. Like that drop of water, you reflect My glory. My light shines from your eyes, because you are in My river. Be yourself. I made you very special, and like your friend told you, 'No one else is better qualified to be you'. That was a word from Me.

Living Stones Vision

I am an infinite God, and I have potential for infinite variety in My creation. My children are all special. All have a place to fill, a role to play as members in My body. Step into your place today. Don't set your affection on things of the earth. Dwell in the heavenly realm. Commit your plans to Me, and I will make your paths straight. I'm with you. You are seated with Me in heavenly places. I have prepared good works for you that you should walk in them. Today, I have a plan for you. My Spirit is within you, and I Myself will do exceeding abundantly above all you can ask or think. Be strengthened with the power of My Spirit. I grant for you to know My love. To comprehend how I love you is the greatest thing. I love you. My love for you is greater, higher, wider and deeper than you can imagine. All this is YOURS, and it's increasing in you. Be strengthened by My Spirit in your inner man, in your heart of hearts."

My Love Makes You a Princess

**Jesus is looking at me with love. I'm a little girl. He puts a little crown on My head and a royal robe on me. It's blue, between sky blue and royal blue, crushed velvet. "You are a princess", He says. "You are not just pretending; even as a little child, you are a princess. I give you authority over ALL the power of the evil one. You don't have to be tall or grown up, because ALL authority has been given to Me, and I give it to you. Believe like a child. Walk in My love. My love makes you a princess. Simple child-like faith is better than thinking you are all grown up and know something. Be a child."

Jesus asks me for the stone in my pocket. I give it to Him, and He places it in my crown. It's like a light blue opal with a light of its own – beautiful! Part of me wants to keep carrying the stone in my pocket, so I can take it out and look at it when I want to. Jesus takes the stone from the crown again and gives it back to me.

Living Stones Vision

"You are a princess," He says, "even when you are playing. The robe and crown are not what make you a princess. My love, the Father's love, and My Holy Spirit within you make you a princess. Be simple and free like a child. You still have authority even as you play. Believe Me, have faith in what I have said. Do the things you see Me and My Father doing. Yes, I healed the sick, I fed the hungry people. I had compassion on those who were as sheep without a shepherd."

Be a Little Child

** Jesus helps me take off my robe and crown. He folds the robe and puts the crown on top and says, "You can put these on whenever you want. Now, run and play".

I'm playing yard games with other children: Crack the Whip, Red Rover, Grey Duck and Simon Says. What fun! Now Jesus gives me a kite to fly. He helps me to launch my kite by running with me till it flies. Then He stands next to me, helping me to hold the kite. "Be a little child, Sweetness. Enjoy life, and play," He says. "Look for opportunities to celebrate. Rejoice and be happy!"

Daughter of the King

"You are a little child," God tells me. "Remember that. But you are also a daughter of the King, My very own daughter. You are a princess. Princess, the angels are your servants and your ministers, because you are My daughter. I give angels charge concerning you to keep you in all your ways" (Psalm 91:11). An angel comes and takes my robe and crown from me to take care of it. I know I can put them on whenever I want, but I'm still a princess without them.

Living Stones Vision

Rest in Me

****I'm with Jesus. We have played and flown the kite, so I'm tired. Jesus hands the kite to an angel, picks me up and carries me to a shady place in the soft grass and lays me down. He covers me with a soft comforter and puts a pillow under my head. "Rest in Me, Sweetness," He says as He gives me a hug and kiss. Then He sits beside me. He puts His hand on my shoulder. "I'm right here, Baby Girl. Go to sleep. I'll speak to you in your dreams and show you what you need to know. Just rest in Me." I'm so comfortable, peaceful and secure, curled up there under the trees with Jesus by my side.

"Find your rest in Me," Jesus says. "Whenever you lack peace, come to Me and rest. It doesn't mean to stop doing everything. I may direct you to work, but I want you to find your peace and rest in Me. Let your soul rest in Me. I love you so much. My love is enough and more than enough to meet all your needs. I am the Bread of Life. I give you the living water of My Spirit. I am your light – the light of the world."

I look at the vision of the bricks again *(see I'm Taking Care of You/ Brick Vision)*. I feel like the Lord says, "Talk to Me; tell me about all the things that you care about. It's okay to just mention these concerns in your prayers. Focus on Me and what I can do – I will take care of them for you. Set your affection on things above, and I will help you with the things below."

Building the House *(It's been a month since I visited the rock in the river with the pile of stones.)*

** I see the river again where Jesus and I collected all the stones. I'm excited, because I know it's time to build the spiritual house! Jesus and I bring the stones to the cornerstone. As soon as the stones

Living Stones Vision

come close to the cornerstone, they connect to the cornerstone like magnets to metal, and they become more like a mountain than a house. My idea of straight walls was way off! The small stones all have flat rounded shapes like perfect skipping stones. I keep putting more stones on and they line up in perfect rows, kind of like round flat bricks as they connect to each other and to the cornerstone. All are different colors, and the light shines through them as they connect to the cornerstone. Beautiful!

The Stone in My Pocket

**I think about my stone in my pocket. I know it can be part of this house or mountain, but I want to keep it. I reach my hand into my pocket. I can feel the stone. "Jesus, do You want me to put my stone on the wall?" I ask. I'm struggling with myself as I think about it. I know I should put it in the house, but I like keeping it with me. I'm reminded of the scripture, "He who has lost his life for My sake will find it".

I take the stone out of my pocket and hand it to Jesus. "Jesus, I give my life to You," I say. Tears come to my eyes as I say it.

Jesus takes the stone and looks at it. "Are you willing for Me to take your life and do what I wish with it? Do you trust Me?"

I'm thinking, "What if He takes it to the lake and tosses it in?" But I know the stone represents my life, and I can trust Jesus with my life.

You Can Trust Me

**Jesus looks at the stone in His hand and smiles, a big, happy, joyful smile, as only He can. "I think I'll keep you right here with Me." He says, looking down at the stone. The stone is in His hand, and He wraps His hand around mine so the stone is in both our hands. "I

Living Stones Vision

hold you in the palm of My hand. You are secure with Me. Precious One, you can always trust Me."

Jesus places the stone back in my hand. I had given it to Him, but now He gives it back. I add it to the wall of the spiritual house, because I know that's what Jesus wants me to do. Jesus and I keep adding stones, but it's easy for me to know which stone is mine — it shines with a blue light, blue like the sky on a clear fall day. Soon my stone is surrounded by many bright colored stones. Beautiful, as living stones, we touch each other, and we touch Jesus, the cornerstone and foundation. The stones are very strong in their magnetic pull toward the foundation and towards each other. They have no such pull if they are away from the cornerstone.

There is no way I could take my stone out of the wall now; it's surrounded by other stones, locked in tightly by the magnetic force around it. Jesus knows what I'm thinking. "Your stone belongs there now," He explains. "Other believers help to hold you close to Me. You add strength to the spiritual house as a living stone. This is a symbol of what happens in the natural. You see how the stones shine brighter once they are connected to the cornerstone and to the other stones. They draw their strength from Me and from each other. I could help you take apart the house so you can get your stone out if you want. But if we leave it here, we can come back and look at it whenever you want. In a sense, you are there, as that stone represents you."

So I say, "No, leave it there; it's beautiful." I touch my blue stone and then the others around it, and I feel strength come into my fingers. The other stones around me represent those closest to me in the body of believers. I can imagine the color of some of the stones: my husband, John (maroon w/gold), my sons David (red) and Peter (dark

Living Stones Vision

green), my sisters Peg (light green) and Jodie (dark pink), friends Joli (golden yellow) and Jeanette (purple, gold & red). Then Jesus shows me how to put a new stone into the wall in a place that's already full of stones, all lined up. He just pushes it in, and the other stones move to make room for it.

"These are living stones," He says. "They are not set like bricks." As soon as He pushes that stone in, it starts to shine, and the stones around it shine brighter, too.

I pick up a stone, "Where should I put it, Jesus?" Jesus looks at the stone. It's white with green, kind of marbled. He points to a spot not far from mine. I push in the stone, and it starts to shine. It belongs to Dean (our new director for East Side Healing Rooms). The stones around it shine brighter. The stones for our team members Rachel, Sid, Cano, Betty, Carl, Lilly, Fred, Peg, Chrysanne, Marsha, Joan, David, John's and mine, and others all shine brighter because of Dean's stone. I look for the stone belonging to Dean's wife Roberta. Jesus hands it to me. It's pink with darker pink or red-violet lights. I push her stone in next to Dean's, and it shines brighter. Dean's stone shines more, and then all the others shine brighter, too. Roberta's stone shines brighter still, because ours are shining.

I'm wondering about what will happen when we move to Mexico. Do we get moved to a different place on the wall of the house? As I think about this, the stones start moving to make room for our stones. There's a fluid-like movement as John's stone and mine move along the rock, staying connected to Jesus the cornerstone. I see that there's still a connection to family and Healing Rooms and Minnesota stones. Like a flow of electricity, but more liquid, strength flows from them to us as we travel. There are stones around us on the other side. Our friends in Mexico: Andrew and Sheryl; Juan and Macrina;

Living Stones Vision

Rafaela, Elias and Imer; Octavio and Guille; Jacinto and Laura and others… All shine brighter when we come; then we shine brighter, too!

Connected By My Spirit

"Is there anything You want to show me about the spiritual house or mountain, Lord?" I ask some days later.

"As a living stone, you draw your strength from Me, but also from other Christians," Jesus answers. "You are not alone. Others draw strength from you. I gave you that vision so you could share it. Write the vision, and make it plain. My body, My spiritual house is all connected by My Spirit with energy, synergy, and magnetism. Christians are drawn to one another and strengthened by one another, especially, those who have been washed in the water of My word, polished by My Spirit. I love you; you are My precious, beautiful child. Life is an adventure; each day is new. My love for you is fresh and bright. Be ready for what I will show you today. Stop from time to time and ask Me. My love and mercy fill you."

Trust Me with Your Heart

"I hold your future in the palm of My hand," Father says. "I'm holding your life right now. Just as in your vision you gave your stone to Jesus and He held it, but then He gave it back to you, so I hold your life, but I give you free choice. I give you free will to do what you want with it. As you give your life to Me, I hold it. I love you and work all things together for good for you. Trust Me with all your heart."

**I'm seeing the spiritual house or mountain again. I'm a little girl about five years old with Jesus in the stream. He sits down on the rock next to the little house. He invites me up on His lap, and I crawl

53

up and snuggle close. "There's strength for those who abide in Me and love one another. My love makes them strong – they are not strong by themselves, but as they receive My love and give it to others, they renew their strength. Stay connected to Me, like the stone in the wall of rocks, and you are connected to many others as well. Your light shines for those outside. Remember the strength you feel when you touch the stones. Last night at the Healing Rooms, as you ministered, you were giving and receiving strength from others."

Washed With the Water of My Word

**I'm back by the stream with Jesus. I take a drink from the stream. Jesus dips His hand and gives me another drink. "Drink," He says. "You need more." It's so wonderful to drink from Jesus hand; He gives me another drink, then another. "You were thirsty," He says. We go over to the mountain of living stones or the spiritual house. We wade in the river to get there. Jesus dips His hand and pours water over the house. Every stone gets brighter and shinier. "My people need to be washed with the water of My word," He says as He pours water over my stone and John's. It feels good, and our stones shine brighter. "Let My words wash over you. Drink them like water. Today, every time you stop to drink, think about My words; drink My words. My rhema words will give life to your soul, spirit and body. Let them wash over you like pure water. Like when you take a shower, it washes off the dirt, dead skin, extra oil and sweat. You smell clean and fresh. My words will do that for your spirit and soul as well as your body. I am the bread of life for you, too. Before you eat, remember that I am your bread."

Living Stones Vision

Be Careful How You Build

"Lord, Father, Holy Spirit," I beg. "I need You so much! I'm thirsty; I need a rhema word, Your Spirit speaking to mine."

**I go down to the stream and lie down on the banks so I can dip in the water to drink. I get up and wade into the stream and sit down in the middle of it. It's about eight inches deep. Now I'm drinking more.

"Drink deeply, Beloved, "Jesus says. He is standing on the bank of the river, watching me and smiling, "Keep drinking. You were so very thirsty."

"Oh, Lord Jesus, speak to me! I need Your words to fill my soul! I need Your words, Daddy God. Open my spiritual eyes and ears. Open my mouth. Fill me with Your Holy Spirit. I'm still thirsty, so thirsty. Speak, Lord; I'm trying to listen."

"Rest in Me," He answers. "Just sit here in My river for a while. Stay; be still and listen. Be patient, and My words will come to you. I love you. Rest in Me. You need Me more than your body needs food or water. It's very important that you take time to listen to Me, to hear My voice. How can you follow Me when you don't wait to see where I'm going? You know My voice, but you have to still yourself to hear it. My Spirit brings you love, joy, peace, patience, kindness, goodness, faithfulness, gentleness (humility) and self-control. Take the time for My Spirit to fill you. Be filled with My Spirit. My Spirit will quench the thirsting of your soul, and you will not be thirsty. Let My love and My Holy Spirit fill you to overflowing. Be careful to build with gold, silver, and precious stones (1Cor. 3:12-14). The gold is My manifest presence. Spend time in My presence, listening to My voice, so you will know how to build. Silver represents redemption. Silver is sharing good news, liberty to the captives, freedom to prisoners, binding up broken hearts" (Isa. 61:1-2).

"Lord," I ask, "what do the precious stones represent? How can I build in precious stones? (Isaiah 54:11-12). I'm thinking of the spiritual house in the stream. Do the precious stones represent the lives of others?"

"Yes," He answers. "When you build someone up, disciple them, or help them to grow, you are building with precious stones. You are a precious stone, and you help others to be built into the wall. In heaven the streets are gold. You are to walk in My manifest presence. In this way, My will is done on earth as it is in heaven. Walk in the awareness of My presence. Abide in Me (Rev. 21:18-20). Stay with Me and walk with Me."

More Stones *(Several months later in Mexico)*

**I'm in the river with Jesus – where we built the spiritual house. "See how the living stones around yours draw strength from Me," Jesus says, "and from each other." So beautiful! Jesús' and Diana's stones are near ours. (Jesús and Diana are our Healing Rooms directors here in Mexico.) Jesús' stone shines golden brown with bright yellow-gold highlights. I think Diana's is purple or a light lilac color with darker streaks. Jesús' stone shines so bright! It has rays coming out from it. It both draws and gives strength to the stones around it. The connection to the cornerstone is also very strong.

Place Your Will in My Hands

**I'm a little girl with Jesus by the river. I'm standing next to Him, and He holds my hand. We're looking up and down the river – up river is the city of God, beautiful but far away. "Remember when you gave Me your stone?" Jesus asks. "Give your life to Me every day like that; place it in My hands. You know you can trust Me. Remember how you were reluctant to put your stone in My house? I want you to surrender your will. Place your will in My hand. I will always give it back to you, but once I've touched it, it will be so much easier for you to do what you know is My will."

Strength of Other Believers (*months later in Minnesota*)

"Precious Daughter," Father says, "I love you. I take care of you. Trust in Me with all your heart. My grace is sufficient for you. Come to Me in your weakness, as a little child."

**I come to Jesus as a five-year-old girl. I want to go to the spiritual "house" on the river. "Yes," Jesus says, "we can revisit that."

I wade over to the rock. To the side is my vase of flowers. I touch the stones on the 'house'. They are so strong, locked in and smooth. I find my stone. It's firmly locked in, and there is light shining from it. It's on the Minnesota side of the mountain again, but there's a pulling and support from the Mexico side. Warmth comes into my little hands as I touch the stones, like the warmth from a coffee cup. I can feel the strength of the stones around me as well as from the cornerstone.

"It was good that you went in to receive prayer on Monday night," Jesus says. "You need the strength of other believers around you. You need to look to them for prayer and support. They will help you."

Living Stones Vision

Linked Together

I feel like I can come back to the place on the river where the little house of living stones is. "Be sure to come as a little child," Jesus says.

**I'm a little child, and I wade into the river so I can look at the house. Jesus is with me. I touch my blue stone. There are some stones around my stone that weren't there a year ago, stones representing team members from our new Healing Rooms location. I feel their strength come into my stone. John and I are more strongly linked together, too. Jesus stands right next to me in the stream. "Lord," I ask, "is there something else You want to show me?"

Jesus smiles... "Do you see that there are so many people that depend on you and you depend on? They all help to keep you connected to Me, and you help them. You are built together. One stone alone could be easily knocked off by the enemy. As you come together in relationship with other believers, you are strong in Me. I'm helping you, and I use other believers to do it."

Chapter 7

Someone Special

You <u>Are</u> Someone Special!

"You are My child," He says, "My very own little girl. Be assured of My love, that you are accepted, that I am pleased with you. My ways are pleasant ways; all My paths are peace, peace between Me and you. You also bring peace to others. Precious One, Sweetness, I send you today to bring My words. Look for the ones I will choose for you to speak to. Listen to My voice, and look to Me."

**At the Holy Spirit Conference: I see myself as a princess, royal, dignified in a beautiful light green dress with a little royal cape and a tiara on my head. I am walking into the conference with my head held high. The angels who are there stand at attention when I walk in, like I'm someone special.

"You <u>are</u> someone special!" Father says. "You are My child, one of My special, gifted children who listen to Me and look to Me."

My Beloved

**I'm 16 years old, the same age I was when I first gave my life to Jesus. I have long hair. Jesus is with me, and He strokes my hair. "Come away with Me, Beloved. Return to your first love with all of your heart. Have the same excitement for Me that you had when you first met Me." Jesus leads me by the hand, and we dance together.

Someone Special

I'm wearing a long muslin dress with embroidery. "You are My Bride, Beloved."

My Love Makes You a Princess

"Ask Me – call to Me, and I will answer you," Father says. "Sweetness, I am setting you free from self-consciousness, free to listen to and obey My voice. Remember that I am <u>with</u> <u>you</u>. My love surrounds you. I set you free to focus on Me and My love for you. My love makes you a princess who knows who the KING is. The King is your Daddy, and you are His precious, much loved child. Be conscious of My great love I have for you. Dance with Me today. Let Me lead you."

Rest in My Arms

**Jesus is holding me. He's down on one knee so that He's at my level as a little child. I'm standing next to Him, and He pulls me close and puts me on His knee. He strokes my hair. "It's alright; you're here with Me, and I love you so much. Just rest in My arms. Draw your strength from me and My love. Let Me carry you today, Precious One. Carry My peace with you."

Drink

**Jesus takes me by the hand and leads me down to the river, and we wade in. "Drink", He says. I cup my hand and drink. We sit down in the river and let the current wash over our legs. "Drink more, till you're full," He says. I cup my hand and keep drinking and keep drinking. I feel so tired and emotionally drained. I lay down in the water and let it wash over my whole body, just my head above the water.

Jesus says, "My words are like water. Let My words wash over you."

Someone Special

(I feel like I should read the book of John. I read and it does wash me like water. I feel better.)

"My words are Spirit and life to you," He says. "I love you and I disclose Myself to you – because you keep My commands, because you love others and listen to My word, and because I love you. You are loved by Me and My Father. We come and make our home with you. We are right here – at home with you. I take care of you. Rest in Me. Abide in Me. Practice My presence."

Your Strength Comes From Me

"Patty, you are a light that shines brightly at your work," He says. "Give Me all your cares about work today. I'm with you. The dream you had reveals your frustration with work. You need to cast all your cares on Me. It's good that you pray for everyone. I'm with you at your work. I will help you with everything – I will help you every moment if you ask Me. Look to Me about your house today as well. I'm with you to help you – ask Me. Cast all your cares on Me, for I care for you. Focus on Me now."

** I'm sitting on Jesus' lap – drawing strength from His embrace. He smiles at Me, and love is in His eyes. "Your strength comes from Me. Rest in Me – in returning and rest shall you be saved. In quietness and in confidence shall be your strength. Those who wait on me renew their strength. You wait on Me – then you can run and not grow weary, because your strength is in Me. Listen to Me, to My voice. I say, 'I love you.' Tune in to Me many times a day. I love you. Listening to Me is true worship."

Someone Special

You Are Not Alone (*At this time I'm working as a nurse's assistant at an Assisted Living Home.*)

**I see myself going in the front door of my workplace, and Jesus is with me with His arm around my shoulders.

"See," Jesus says, "My arm is around you when you go into work. You are not alone. I'm with you as you touch and help each person – I am touching them and helping them, as well, through you. I love them through you. I care about each one. I am there with you to give you strength and guidance. I fill you with My Spirit."

Love, Joy, and Peace

"I love you, Baby Girl," Father tells me. "You are Mine. I'm with you, yes, right here and now."

"Would You fill me with Your love now?" I beg. "I'm thirsty for You, for more of You."

"Yes, Let My presence fill you, My love, joy and peace."

** I see **love** like the red liquid hearts I've seen in my vision before. Then I asked, "What does **joy** look like?" I see bubbles. Jesus is blowing bubbles with me! I think I need to buy some bubbles. **Peace** is like the sunset on the lake last night. It's so beautiful – silver and pink and blue in the sky and on the water.

The City

**Jesus takes me by the hand and leads me. We're walking along the banks of the river. He's bringing me to the city of God. "The river comes from My city; from under the throne of God. You will live in My city, and in a sense you are already here. Yes, it's beautiful. Stay

Someone Special

in a place of beautiful fellowship with Me and My Father. Remember that My Spirit is within you."

Washing Feet

**Jesus is washing the disciples' feet, then washing my feet as well. Then He says, "Do you know what I have done to you? I am your Lord and Master; I'm your teacher, and I wash your feet – you ought to wash one another's feet. This is a mystery that I want you to understand. I am your teacher. Be patient, and I will reveal to you these mysteries" (John 13:1-18).

"How can I do this, Lord?" I ask. "How do I wash another's feet?"

"You are light," Jesus answers. "The light that is in you shines on them, so they can see where they are dirty. Many of My children don't realize just how dirty their feet have become from walking in this world. You don't need to point out their faults – My light will show them up. They need to be washed with the water of My word. My words are Spirit and life. You know the RHEMA words I have spoken to your heart. These words will bring life to others and will wash their spiritual feet. I have washed your feet, and you are clean.

"Washing feet is not a pleasant task, but when you do it in love, it becomes something beautiful and wonderful. You must humble yourself, as I did, in order for it to be effective. Patty, I am blessed that you have humbled yourself to do the humble work of a nurse's aide. My disciples' feet were very dusty and dirty. You know how it can be walking about in the dusty roads of the dry season in Mexico, and how good it feels to wash your feet. This is how it was – but none of My disciples had humbled themselves to do this lowly task. This was an everyday task for the lowest servant. I am meek and lowly of heart. Have this attitude, and you will be like Me. Pride has no place in foot washing. The words I have spoken to your heart will wash others feet. If you confess your sins, I am faithful and just to forgive your sins and cleanse you from all unrighteousness (I John 1:9). Wash others' feet out of love for Me. Even as Mary kissed My feet, washed them with her tears, dried them with her hair and anointed them with perfume (John 12:3, Luke 7:37-47). When you love the lowly ones in My body, you are kissing My feet. I showed you this before – remember it. This is a mystery revealed. Love the unlovely of My body out of love for Me. Mary was aware of how much I have forgiven her, and so she loved Me much. This is how you are to wash others' feet, out of love for Me. Care for their needs, and love them."

Like a Tree

"Precious One, I'm here with you," God says. "My mercies are new every morning; new today. I love you so much. My love for you is EVERLASTING. I have always loved you – that's why I created you."

"What do You want me to know today?" I ask.

"You are becoming a mature believer," Father answers. "You are like a tree, and others will rest under your shade. To be planted, steady, immovable – standing, rooted and grounded in My love, you must be filled with My peace. Abide in Me, and you are like a tree planted by streams of water. Let your roots go down deep into the soil of My love. As you mature, you bear fruit, and others can eat of your fruit and be satisfied. A tree is also flexible – it bends and moves with the wind; its leaves clap their hands in praise to Me. You are a blessing to Me and to others. Your delight is in Me and My words; you meditate on My words day and night. Your leaf does not wither; your leaves are for healing. Whatever you do prospers. If you stay close and abide in Me, you will have great success, and whatever you do will

Someone Special

prosper (Psalm 1:1-3). As you rest under the shade of the trees, and walk with me among the trees, you draw strength to grow to maturity. I have called you to come apart with Me and draw from Me, to meditate on the words I have given you. You will bear fruit in your old age, because I renew your strength. You will bear fruit in season. Even now, some of your fruit is ripening, and other fruit is just starting to form. Some of your fruit is in the flower stage. Keep drinking from My river, and the miracle of My fruit will appear, the kind of fruit in Galatians: love, joy, peace, patience, kindness, goodness, faithfulness, gentleness, and self-control" (Galatians 5:22-23).

Jesus Comes Into Church

(At church before service in the prayer room: Someone prays, "God, open our eyes so we can see You...")

**Jesus is walking in the front door of the church, coming around to each person and smiling, beaming at people. I love the way He walks with a bounce in His step, a little playful, laughing with and smiling at us. He greets people as they come in and hugs everyone who will hug Him. He makes sure He greets everyone and is so happy that we are here. I see Him going to give Pastor Denny a hug and a touch as He finishes preparing his sermon. Then He touches the shoulders of those in the back of the sanctuary as they sit in their chairs. Jesus is so happy to be here in our church and happy that we are here today.

Talk to Me/ In the River

"Keep those running conversations with Me going," God says. "Listen for My voice, and tell Me about what you're doing. Talk to Me about the things that concern you. Give Me all your burdens. I love you. Seek My kingdom and My righteousness. Look for ways My kingdom needs to come into your life. Look for Me in every situation. Focus on Me and My words. I bring joy, light and love to you, and you bring it to others. I bring My peace to you, and you bring it to others."

I ask, "Is there anything You want me to see? Open the eyes of my heart."

** I'm sitting in the river, letting the water run over my legs. I'm resting and relaxing in the rushing water, watching the water, enjoying the sunshine and the beautiful day. Jesus is with me. The water is clear and rushing. It's a little like the water paradise we visited in Uruapan, Michoacán, Mexico. The water is bright like it has a light of its own that shines from within. I'm enjoying the sound of the rushing waters and the peace of this place and being with Jesus here. Jesus says, "Come to this place when you need peace today. Find your peace and rest in me."

Come to the Waters

"Sweetness, I am with you," Jesus says. "Never do I ever leave you. I'm with you always even when you may be unaware of My presence. Dwell in My river. Let My anointing cover you and bring life. Throughout the day, you can come back to My river. Let My waters refresh your soul. Are you thirsty? Come to the waters. Listen carefully to Me, eat what is good and delight your soul in abundance. Turn your ear to Me, come to Me; listen that you may live. Seek Me, call upon Me. My thoughts and ways are higher than yours. Look for Me, call on Me and listen; and you will hear My thoughts and words for wherever you find yourself. Let My living water flow over you like a waterfall. I'm with you always. Drink My words. Let My living water refresh your soul" (Isaiah 55:1-13).

Someone Special

I'm Right Here

"Sweetness, Precious One, I'm right here with you," Father says. "Let Me fill you with My strength. I love you with My everlasting love. I will use you today to show My love to people. Let Me help you today: always keep in mind that I'm with you to help you. Give Me your heart, and I give you a new heart; My heart beats in yours in the same rhythm. You need Me for comfort and strength; rest in Me even as you work. Find your peace in Me. Precious Child, you are My very own. Breathe Me in. I fill you now. My blessing is all over you. You need Me to help you. You can do nothing without Me. Abide in Me; stay close to Me. Not by might nor by power but by My spirit. Not of your own ability – stay connected to Me like a branch to a vine."

Vision of Cuernavaca, Mexico

(This is shortly before our return to Mexico in 2009 after three years in the USA.)

"Hello, Sweetness," Father says. "How are you?"

"I'm happier than I've ever been because of You, God," I answer. "Your love has made me so happy. Thank You, God."

"There's more," He says. "I will set you free from all that has bound you in the past. I have many things to teach you. (John 16) You are on a journey, an adventure. I reveal things to you that are especially prepared just for you (1 Cor. 2:9-16). You have My Spirit within you to teach you. I guide you into all TRUTH. You will know the truth; you will know Me, and I set you free. So then you have My mind on any matter that you ask me about. Also there are things you never thought of that I want you to know."

Someone Special

**Jesus is with John and me. We're walking through deep woods with pine trees. We come to a clearing, and there's a city in a valley. It looks like Cuernavaca, because there are mountains all around. Jesus says, "I have many people in this city, people who are sick and hurting. I'm bringing you here. These three years I have been preparing you, and you are almost ready for the work I've prepared for you."

**A few days later, I come back to this vision. I see the city and its suburbs more clearly. It is Cuernavaca. It stirs up such emotion in me. Jesus says, "You and John are bringing My love and healing to this city. Many are hurting and wounded and don't know what to do. You bring My love and healing to them. I will show you how. Many will be released into ministry."

I see a Mexican couple who are in ministry there in Cuernavaca, friends of ours. I see the Lord taking scales off of her eyes and chains from her arms, setting her free. She falls back and rests in a cloud. I see University students coming to receive from God. I say, "I don't know how to minister to young people."

Jesus replies, "You won't have to; I have people in place, and I will minister to them."

Be Strong and Courageous

(We are on the way driving down to Mexico in the fall and are now in New Braunfels, Texas.)

"My love for you is greater, higher, wider, longer and deeper than you can imagine," God says. "I love you so much. Have I not commanded you? Be strong and courageous! Do not tremble or be dismayed, for the Lord your God is with you wherever you go (Josh.

Someone Special

1:9). Every place on which the sole of your foot treads, I have given it to you (Josh. 1:3). You will be winning territory for Me."

Cuernavaca Vision *(continued)*

**I see Jesus with His arms around John and me as we come walking out of the woods into the city of Cuernavaca. "Go! I go with you as you take possession of the land. Know that I am sending you and I am with you. You are bringing My peace, love and healing to people. You bring My kingdom. Arise, shine; for your light has come, and the glory of the Lord has risen upon you" (Isa. 60:1).

Rest in My Love

"I'm here with you," Jesus says. "I love you so much. My arms are around you. I'm here with you in your kitchen, and in the spirit you are a little girl curled up on My lap with My arms around you. You need My touch and My embrace. See? I'm touching your spirit now. My love fills you. Rest in My love."

**Jesus strokes my hair and breathes in the scent of it. He squeezes my arm. "You are so beautiful and precious to Me. You are My sweet, precious little girl. Let go of all guilt. I forgive your sins and remove them from you. You are innocent and clean, fresh and sweet, like a little girl. My light shines on you. You've confessed what I've shown you, and that's enough. I cleanse you from ALL unrighteousness" (1 John 1:9).

Jesus Conquered the Giants

> Joshua 15:16-19: And Caleb said, "The one who attacks Kiriath-sepher and captures it, I will give him Achsah my daughter as a wife." Othniel the son of Kenaz the brother of

Someone Special

Caleb, captured it: so he gave him Achsah his daughter as a wife.

It came about that when she came to him she persuaded him to ask her father for a field. So she alighted from the donkey, and Caleb said to her, "What do you want?"

Then she said, "Give me a blessing; since you have given me the land of the Negev, give me also springs of water." So he gave her the upper springs and the lower springs.

Father says this to me about it, "Like Othniel, Jesus conquered the giants to win your hand as His Bride. I give you a field to work, to you and to all who ask for it. And you ask Me, your Father for springs of water, so you can water your land. I freely give you the upper and lower springs, more than what you ask for. The land represents ministry; ask Me and I give you ministry. The springs of water represent My anointing and supply. Ask Me for them; I Am your provider, and I will provide more than you need, but I wait for you to ask. You are a princess, the daughter of a king. You are part of the beautiful Bride for My Son Jesus."

Floating

"Sweetness, I've been waiting for you to come," He says. "I love it when you draw near. Draw near My love."

**Jesus takes me swimming in the lake by the stream. We're floating on our backs, looking up at the clouds. "Rest in me, like floating in a lake. Just lean back and let yourself float. Let go of trying to figure things out. Today keep this vision in your spirit and heart. Lean back on Me and rest. Look at the clouds. I'm with you, Baby Girl; I love you."

Someone Special

Drink Deeply

"I'm with you, My child," Jesus says. "I'm holding your hand and watching over you. You are Mine. I give you to drink; you are so thirsty."

**Jesus and I are sitting on the bank of the stream with our feet in the rushing water. He cups His hand and dips and gives me a drink from His hand of the cool refreshing water. "Drink deeply, Beloved. Come to Me and drink whenever you are thirsty. Drink deeply of My living water. I love you; I'm with you. Don't trust your feelings; trust Me with all your heart and do not lean on your own understanding (Prov. 3:5). Come closer to Me. Listen, there are things I want to tell you, but you haven't been listening. I want to fill you so full that you overflow with My living water. To you it has been given to know the secret things, the mysteries I want to reveal to you. I pour out My Spirit on you with a reason and for a purpose. Precious One, I love you. Let My wonderful, beautiful love fill you. My love is a wonder. I want you to know it more. Trust Me with your whole heart. Be filled with My love. My love is the greatest, most important thing. You still need to know it more; how much I love you. You need to be filled up to all My fullness. I am able to fill you so that you thirst no more. Come into the depth of My love. I want you to know the breadth and length and height and depth. Sweet Girl, My love is the most important thing, the greatest thing. Drink more, receive more, and be filled with it. My love makes you a princess, My precious child, My very own daughter.

"You are here with Me in heaven seated on the throne with Me, next to My Father and yours. You need not wait for the rapture. Be enveloped by My love. Look not at the things which are seen but at the things which are not seen. These things are eternal. My love for you is eternal. I always love you; I always will. The heavenly city is yours. You are already here with Me. There is more beauty here than you can possibly imagine. More beautiful than the most beautiful place you have ever been on earth. I want you to see it, just as you saw your white heavenly robes. See the city. Come up higher. Let me use your imagination."

Think About the City

Set your affection on things above, not on things of the earth (Col. 3:1). Father says, "Think about the city; it's beautiful and full of light. You have come to the city of God. Live in My city. My city is both present and future. It has not physically come to earth, but as part of My Bride, you are already there. Because I am with you, you are filled with light. Your light shines. The Jerusalem above is free; she is your mother (Gal.4:26). You are born again, born of the Spirit. The heavenly city is your home."

"Lord," I say, "I want to see it, the heavenly city."

"You have the description in Revelation 21 and Isaiah 60," Father says. "See it in your mind's eye; live here in your spirit. When you listen to My words, you are drinking from My river. You are washed by My words, and I clothe you in fine linen, bright and clean, heavenly white. I clothe you in garments of salvation and praise; I wrap you with a robe of righteousness (Isa.61:10). You are beautiful, My child, Precious One. You shine for Me. I will help you to see the city and better, to live in My city where I Am your light."

My Rhythm

"Come up here," Father says. "Know that as surely as you are sitting on a chair in your kitchen, you are seated with Me in heaven. I raised

Someone Special

you up with Jesus and you ascended with Him, and here you are with Me, seated on My throne. My throne has lots of room, many dwelling places. You, Sweetness, have a special place in My heart. Let your heart beat in Mine. Be still, Child. If I told you to be here to feel the rhythm of My heart, you can be assured that you will, you do, and you are here in My heart. Peace, be still. Hear the rhythm around you. Hear the doves cooing; they echo My rhythm. Hear people walking; their footsteps as they walk echo My rhythm. The birds beat their wings in rhythm to fly. Even the cars and trucks have to have timing and rhythm in order to function. The washing machine and refrigerator use rhythm. Men tapped into the secret to make their machines. My heart beats with a special rhythm, but remember My heart whenever you hear or see rhythm around you. Let it be a reminder of how My heart beats in yours, in your body, soul and spirit. My heart says, 'I love you, I love you, I love you so much, so much, so much.' Yes, see the rhythm in the bush as the branches sway in My breeze. My rhythm is all around you, in every movement. The way your hand moves your pen on the page; there is rhythm there. I tell you this so you will remember to think of Me throughout the day today. Even now, the sounds can all help you to center on Me. You need not be distracted by noises. The rhythms of heaven are beautiful, with perfect harmony, but the rhythms of earth reflect them. Like the crickets chirp in the summer, all of My creation reflects My rhythm and harmony."

I'm Going Before Them

"Lord," I ask, "is there something You want me to know about the team coming for the conference?" *(Four people from Tijuana are coming here to Cuernavaca to teach a Healing Rooms conference in December 2009.)*

Someone Special

"I'm going before them," Jesus answers. "When I put forth My own sheep, I go before them" (John 10:4).

** Jesus is in the plane, getting things ready for the team. He dusts off their seats and checks the cargo bins. He goes into the cockpit and lays hands on the pilot and co-pilot. Then He checks all the dials and gadgets. I see Him outside checking the landing gear, the engines, and the baggage compartment. He goes out to the runway and walks the runway where the plane will take off. Then I see Him on the ground in Mexico City, doing the same, walking the runway. Inside the Mexico City airport, I see Him lay hands on the people who will help them. I see Him get into the bus they will take, laying His hands on the seats they will sit on. He lays His hands on the driver and on the engine. There are three angels posted on the bus; two in front, one in back.

Chapter 8

Waterfall Vision

You Need More Of Me

"I'm here, Baby Girl," Father says. "Yes, you need more of Me. More, I want to fill you more. I want you to know My love that surpasses all knowledge, that you may be filled up to all My fullness. I am able to do far more abundantly beyond all that you ask or think, according to the power that works within you (Ephes. 3:20). I give you more of Me today. You need more of Me, more and more, like a waterfall."

**Jesus brings me into a waterfall about 20 feet high and five feet wide. He and I are standing under it and getting all wet and laughing. Then I step out, and I'm shaking the water off my hands and hair and clothes, but Jesus pulls me back in!! "You need more," He says, "more of My glory, My refreshing and power."

It's so much fun! I think, "Others should be enjoying this!" so I bring my sons Peter and David, then my husband John, then many other friends. The more people come in, the wider and stronger the waterfall is, just blasting us. I have to stand back behind the water, and watch because it is so strong and hard to just stand right in it. I still get really sprayed standing behind. Peter is running through it back and forth, laughing. John is jumping up and down for joy, dancing in circles. Everyone is laughing, and David, I don't know how he does it, but he stays under the full force of the water just getting blasted. Now everyone keeps bringing more people in, and the

Waterfall Vision

waterfall gets bigger and wider. Jesus is so happy!! *(Dear reader, step in now and get refreshed!!!)*

More People = Greater Blessing

"Listen to Me for a while, first thing," Jesus says. "You remember the waterfall? That's how I am; I want you to be happy. I pulled you back in, because you needed more. You invited others in, because you want others to be happy and blessed, too. Come with Me now. The more people who come in, the greater the blessing is."

**I'm at the waterfall with Jesus. I'm inviting more people to come in and bringing them: Juan and Macrina, our Pastor and his wife; Rafaela, Elias and Imer, our Christian neighbors; Ricky, Raul, Ivan, Vero, Pablo and Moises, the worship team; my Mom and Dad and Peg, Jodie and Jerry, more family. I can see the reaction of each one. My Dad hangs back and watches, but he's having fun watching others get really wet, and he's smiling. Mom stands close to the edge of the falls and puts her hand in the water. Jodie and Jerry are both standing, leaning against the rock wall. *(Note: Jerry is my brother-in-law, who is physically paralyzed from the neck down, so it's nice to see him standing in my vision.)* Then Jerry leans his head into the blast of water. Jesus comes and pulls Jodie and Jerry into the waterfall, and they are both strengthened.

"I am come that you may have life and have it more abundantly," Jesus says.

Jesus takes my two hands in His. He's on one side of the falls, and I'm on the other, and He pulls me through the blast of water. Then He gives me a big wet hug. *(Something is happening in my spirit and my emotions as I see this, because the tears are really flowing now.)* Now Jesus starts jumping up and down for joy! He holds both of my hands, and He gets me jumping in circles in and out of the water. Then He goes to each person, whoever will jump, and He does the same, pulling them through the waterfall, hugging some of them and getting them to jump. Not everyone is ready; some are still just watching. But soon there are lots of people jumping in and out of the water fall. My sons and their friends are all jumping and having a great time.

Our pastor Juan seems a little hesitant at first till Jesus pulls him through the water, gives him a big smile and hug, and then starts jumping with him. Soon Juan is jumping and laughing, too, and then his wife Macrina and the whole worship band. Jesus gives Ricky (our blind guitar player) an especially tender hug. Then Jesus takes him by the arms with His hands on His elbows and starts him jumping and dancing in the waterfall. As I look again, Ricky has His guitar, and he's jumping with the guitar, but it doesn't seem to matter that it gets wet.

Now everyone brings more friends and family members. Some of them hang back against the rock wall, just watching, but everyone is smiling or laughing. Jesus comes by and greets each one who is hanging back, giving each one a handshake and a big smile if they aren't ready for a hug or to come in to the waterfall. He doesn't pull anyone in if they're not ready. Those who are watching can't help but smile; there's a sense of wonder, too. Again, the more people who gather, the wider and stronger the waterfall becomes.

Just You and Me

"Let's go to the waterfall again," Jesus says. *(Some weeks later)*

Waterfall Vision

** I'm with Jesus, and He brings me to the waterfall. He pulls me under the waters. We're both standing on a rock ledge where the water is falling on us, and we're laughing.

"Stay here a while, just you and Me," Jesus says. "Enjoy the experience alone with Me. Don't try to see more right now; don't strive. I'm with you – just enjoy My company and drink." I open my mouth and step under the waterfall. I drink the water. It's cold and sweet and refreshing. Jesus takes me in His arms and gives me a hug. "This is what you need most right now, to be with Me, drinking in My words. Listen to My voice. I'm here. I love you. Each [Healing Rooms] team member needs this too. The special time you spend alone with Me will affect the time you spend with others. Yes, you can invite whomever you wish to come in to My waterfall, but first let's enjoy it together, just you and Me. Drink more – get in the water more."

Precious Daughter

Chapter 9

Precious Daughter

Rest Like a Little Child

"I'm here with you," God says. "Rest in Me, and wait on My words for a time. After this week with all the hours you've put in, you need rest. Rest in Me, Sweetness. Cast your cares on me. My joy is your strength. Honor Me by listening to Me now. I will help you with everything this week. Rest today. Princess, My angels strengthened My Son. Do you think I would do less for you? Be a little child. Hold My hand and let Me love you. Rest with Me in My garden."

**I'm sitting as a little girl with Jesus on the bank of the stream in the heavenly garden. Our bare feet are in the stream. He strokes my hair. "Precious Little One, I love it when you come to me as a little child." There are pretty little birds flying all around, and singing in the trees. Beautiful!

A little blue bird brings a ribbon and drops it in my lap. It's blue satin. Jesus ties it into a perfect bow and hands it back to me. "Can we put it in my hair?" I ask.

Jesus ties the bow into my hair. "Precious One, you are so beautiful and sweet. Let My light shine from your eyes, and others can get a little glimpse of heaven. Live in heaven even during your time on earth. Be filled with heaven. Set your affection on things above, not on things on the earth. It's okay that you don't see really clearly. Keep looking. You will see the things I want you to see. "

On Jesus' Lap

**I'm a little girl sitting on Jesus lap, and He hugs me. I receive His love. He kisses me on my cheeks. I'm drinking in His love and His touch as a little baby drinks in her mother's love and touch.

I'm Taking You to Where You need to Be

**I come to Jesus as a little girl. He takes my hand, and we walk together down to the stream. We walk alongside the stream together. The grass is green, and there are trees and flowers and blue sky. Jesus stoops down and picks me up and whirls me around in circles till I'm laughing and dizzy. He sets me down, but I lift up my hands, so He picks me up again and carries me. We walk along the stream, Jesus carrying me, till we see a mountain. The mountain looks close, but it's really far away. Jesus runs fast to get to the base of the mountain quickly, still carrying me, and He starts climbing the mountain, going up a steep path. We get halfway up and stop at an overlook where we can see for miles. There's a valley and more mountains and hills. There's a city in the valley.

(Later, I ask God what this vision means. "I am taking you very quickly to where you need to be," He answers. "Be like a little child, and let me carry you. Soon you will be able to see things more clearly; where you are going and where you've been.")

My Heart Beats in Yours

"Precious Daughter, come close," Father says. "I want to be with you. I want you to pay attention to Me and My words now. I want to speak to you heart-to-heart, so that My heart beats in yours, and so

Precious Daughter

your heart beats in My rhythm. I love you. Today is a new day I have created for you. My love and mercy are new every morning. So when I say 'I love you,' that love is new and beautiful, like a new fresh flower which just opened today. My love for you is beautiful and much greater than you think. My love is perfect, and it brings comfort and peace. It casts out all fear. You can be so secure when you just rest in My love. Let me take care of you like a little child. Be a little child with Me. Rest in Me. Baby Girl, I'll show you what to do and when to do it, if you keep on looking to Me."

Let Me Love You

"I love you," Jesus says. "Be still and listen now. Sit here with Me for a while. Just be with Me. Sit on My lap, and let Me hold you close. Let Me love you. It's okay; you don't have to do anything. Just be a little child, and let Me hold you and love you."

** I'm a little baby, about one year old, on Jesus' lap. I turn and wrap my arms around His neck and lay my head on His shoulder. He holds me close and hugs me. "That's right," He says. "What you need most is to receive My love. Be a little baby girl, knowing that I'm caring for you and protecting you. You are so very safe in My arms."

Drink My Words

"Beautiful, you are beautiful to Me, and you are My very own daughter," He says. "I love you so much. Come to me, and drink My words. Let them go into your innermost being. Let My words kiss you on the mouth."

"Yes, Lord," I reply. "May You kiss me with the kisses of Your mouth, for Your love is better than wine. Your mouth is full of sweetness, and You are wholly desirable" (Song of Sol. 1:2, 5:16).

Precious Daughter

"I love you so much," Jesus says. "My love is better than any other pleasure you can imagine. Come close, and receive My love. My love is pure, Precious One."

** I'm a little girl in my blue T-shirt and pants, and I crawl up on Jesus' lap, and He holds me. His love pours into me. "This is what you need most, Precious One," He says. "You need me to hold you; you need My love to fill you more. Whenever you come to Me and let Me hold you, My blessing fills you more. As a little child needs to be held close to his mother, and his body, soul, and spirit drink in his mother's love, even so you need My closeness. It's so important to your development; spiritually, emotionally, and physically. This is why you so often see yourself as a little child on My lap. You need My love. You need more. There are no limits to how much of Me you can receive. There's always more. There won't come a day when you are as full as you will ever be. My love is new every morning. Every day I give you greater capacity if you will come close and receive it. So you are on My lap now; receive My love. Look in My eyes as a little one drinks in love by looking into his mother's eyes."

You Hold My Hand

**I'm a little girl on Jesus' lap, and He holds me and sings to me, "Draw near to Me..." Then He sets me down and takes me by the hand, and we start walking. The grass is so green and soft, and we're barefoot. We walk beside the stream, and the sun is warm. "Walk with Me, stay close and hold My hand today, and I will show you what to do. I love you so much. Just stay close to Me in all you do today. Keep that awareness that you hold My hand. I watch over you. I take care of you. You are Mine."

Precious Daughter

Stay With Me

"Waiting on Me and listening to Me are so important, because in this time with Me I give you your identity," He says. "This is how you have come to know who you are, and who I Am. Every day I tell you that I love you, because you need to know it. I tell you who you are – My precious, beautiful child, a princess in My kingdom. Many believers spend much time reading My word, but they don't get this concept. I keep telling you to stay close to Me. Do this! Be a doer of My word and not a hearer only. Abide in Me; stay with Me. Be aware of My presence. I'm with you."

Get All Wet in My Holy Spirit

"I'm with you," Father says. "My presence is more precious than gold. My words are pure, like silver refined and purified seven times in a furnace (Psalms 12:6). Call to Me, and I will answer you. I will tell you great and mighty things that you do not know (Jer. 33:3). I love you, Baby Girl. You are Mine – so precious and beautiful."

I'm watching our neighbor playing with his nephews, running and laughing; so precious and fun. Jesus says, "I am like that – I love to have fun and play. Be like a little child. Laugh and play. I love you, Baby Girl."

**I'm in the river with Jesus. I'm about nine years old; we're standing in the water above the falls and we can see the city afar off like Mount Popo *(the volcano that's about 30 miles away)*. Jesus splashes me, and I splash back. Soon we're all wet and laughing. Jesus lifts me and throws me into the water, as my dad used to do when I was small.

Precious Daughter

I come back and say, "Again!" He picks me us and tosses me in again. The water temperature is just right, and the air is warm. The sun is shining in the blue sky, and the trees and grass are so green.

"When you minister, it can be like this." Jesus says. "Just stay with Me in My river. Stay in My presence, and make sure you are with Me. Get all wet in My Holy Spirit."

I Place a Rod in Your Hands

"As you read today, stop and listen to what I'm saying," Father says. "Write what you hear from Me. Moses was on the hill holding My staff. The work of the battle was there. Joshua and his army were fighting below, and yes, they have to fight, but the success of the battle depended on Moses (Ex. 17:8-13).

"You are in a battle for this area of Mexico. Moses had one staff, and with this same staff came mercy and judgment. Moses struck the rock with it, and out came rivers of water. Cool and sweet and clean. Jesus was stricken by the religious leaders of His day, and from Him came living water. By My mercy, I place a rod in your hands. Hold it up high, like a banner.

"Prayer is the most important thing. These people must fight, but prayer is what you will find as the key, a banner to encourage all those who fight. The rod represented the great things I had already done for them: the judgments on Egypt, the opening of the Red Sea and the water from the rock. Remember what great things I have already done for you and for this people. Hold these things up as a banner, and the battle will go well. I have brought you here to Cuernavaca for a reason and a purpose. I have called you to be like Moses, to hold My banner high in prayer. Lift up Jesus so all can see, and they will be encouraged in the battle. You represent Me here.

Precious Daughter

Like Moses, you may become weary, but I send help to hold up your hands. Don't let down your hands; continue to lift Me up. If you get weary, ask for help, but don't let down your hands. This is very simple. Keep close to Me, lift Me up, and give Me the glory for every battle won. We will win.

"The battle is Mine. I am with you to help you. Be strong and of good courage – do not fear or be afraid. I will fight for you. I have never left you. Do not fear or shrink back. Keep listening for My words and My voice. I will speak to you whenever you listen. Remember that perfect love casts out all fear. I love you with My perfect love."

I Take Care of You

"I am come that you might have life and have it more abundantly," Jesus says. "Come with Me now. Wait on Me; wait for Me. Be still, and focus on Me. You are in a different stage of your life when you can focus on Me more. I want to fill you with My love, Sweetness. You are very special and precious to Me, My very own lovely daughter. I love you so very much. Be filled to overflowing with My love. Sit here on My lap for a while, and just enjoy My embrace. Like a baby – you need to be touched and loved and held close."

**I'm a little one, about one year old, and Jesus is holding me, carrying me just like my neighbor carries his granddaughter. "Stay here in My arms, and just let Me hold you. You need My love most of all." We walk along in the garden, and He shows me the flowers and pretty birds. Just like this morning, I looked at the pretty robins and blue-grey gnatcatcher and the yellow warblers. "Look at how I take care of the birds – in the trees I provide food and shelter for them, even the little common house sparrows. I care for you much more than for them. I take care of you. You don't need to worry or strive. Just rest in My arms, and be blessed. Let My blessing fill you."

Precious Daughter

Give All Your Time to Me

"Like the altar of incense overlaid with pure gold, your time of prayer needs to be offered on an altar of pure gold," God says. "Make sure you come into My presence. Your prayer time is not rote and ritual but needs to be offered on the altar of My presence. I have called you to prayer, to intercession, and this includes hearing My voice. Your prayer is like incense of the purest spices, fragrant, a pleasing aroma to Me. This is your calling; to intercede, to listen and pray" (Ex. 37:25-29).

Offer your prayer time as a sacrifice – costly; costing you your time. Because I love you and you can be filled with My love, your sacrifice will be a beautiful thing. It will bring you much joy – it will bring joy to others as well. Don't hold time as being your own, but give Me your whole life – surrender. This is important work, the most important thing you do. Make your life a whole burnt offering – everything subject to My purifying fire, My judgment (bronze altar). I call you to complete surrender. Patty, hold nothing back from Me; give all your "free" time to Me, all of it. "

"I don't know how to do this, Lord," I say. "I offer it to You now, but I know how I am. I'm selfish, and I confess this as sin, Father. Part of me wants to take it back. But I'm willing to give it all to You. Cleanse me from this sin. Let my life be a whole burnt offering, without spot or blemish. I confess my unwillingness, Lord. I'm not faithful, but You are faithful to forgive me and cleanse me from all unrighteousness" (1 John 1:9).

** I remember my vision of when I gave my stone to Jesus by the river. He handed it back to me, because I knew what He wanted me to do with it.

Precious Daughter

"It's the same with your time, Sweetness," God answers. "I give it back to you, because you already know what to do. When you don't know, ask Me, and I will show you."

Run to Me When I Call

"I'm with you, Beautiful One," Father says to me. "Just relax. Rest in Me, and allow Me to speak to you. I love you, and you are My beloved daughter. I have called you; stay close to Me."

** Jesus calls me out of a crowd of little ones playing in a field. "Patty!" He shouts. I come running into His arms. He hugs me, then sets me on my feet and takes my hand. We start walking up the side of the stream. "Stay close by so you can come whenever I call, Patty. I will be calling you to walk closer with Me. Be like a little child, and run to Me when I call."

The City is Your Home

"Drink from My living water; it comes from My throne." Jesus tells me. "My words are life and water for your soul. Rest with Me beside still waters."

**I'm sitting beside Jesus by the stream as a small child, and He gives me a cup – a pottery cup. He dips it in the stream for me, and I drink. I'm really thirsty, so I drink it down quickly. He dips it again and hands it to me. I drink again. While I'm drinking, He strokes my hair and my shoulder. "You need more, Sweetness," He says. "Keep drinking; I give you heavenly drink. I want you to be full of Me and My words." A third time – "Drink, Baby Girl, drink more of Me. This river comes right from My throne and My Father's throne. It is the water of My Holy Spirit and of My words. I give you to drink from the pottery cup, made from the clay of the earth. Keep learning from My earthly life. There is so much that I want you to know. My Spirit will show you My ways."

I go into the river with Jesus and wash my face and hands. "Now you're ready," He says. "Come with me." Jesus takes me by the hand, and we walk along the stream. The sun is shining, and I can see the city far away. I can't see it very well; it's so far off and not very clear. It's like a mountain of columns, light purplish in color like quartz. It shines with a golden light from within. I want to see it more clearly and closer. Jesus says, "You are getting closer. The city is your home. You have a place there. You are part of My Bride. I have prepared it for you, and I have touched every part of it: every building, every street, every room, every tree and flower. In a sense, you have already seen and touched it – spiritually you are already there. John (the beloved) saw and described it so you could imagine what it's like. You've been drinking from the water that runs beside its streets. Be like Mary, and keep listening to My words (Luke 10:39). Keep your focus on Me, and like Mary, you will know what to do and when. It may not seem right to others around you, as when Mary poured out the perfume on My feet and wiped My feet with her hair, but it will be exactly the right thing (John 12:3). The key is to have a hearing heart."

"Is there more You want to say to me?" I ask.

"Just be with Me a while longer," He says.

** I crawl up on Jesus' lap, and He holds me. My head is on His chest, and He strokes my hair. "Rest in Me," He says. "Receive My love. Don't strive; just be close to Me. My love is what you need most." I feel like something is being touched and healed deep inside as Jesus holds me. The tears are flowing, and I'm overcome with emotion.

Precious Daughter

Listening to Me

"You are My precious child, My very own daughter, from My family," He says. "You belong to Me – I created you and formed you. I also watched over you when you were far away from Me in your heart. I loved you then, too. You were in My heart, and I longed for you to come close. Look to Me. I see you, what you will become. Listening to Me is the most important thing. Focus on Me and My words. Sweetness, be here with Me. Drink from My stream of living water. Eat My words."

**Jesus and I are sitting on the bank of the stream, and now He points to the grass behind us. There is manna on the grass! I turn and pick some up and eat it. "When you listen carefully to My words, it's like food for your spirit and soul. My words become part of you, and give you strength" (Isa. 55:2).

I Have Great Plans For You

**"You need more time with Me," Jesus says. "Take this time today to get full of Me and My love. You're thirsty. Come to My river and drink from My hand," I'm with Jesus by the river, and He dips into the river and gives me a drink, then another, and another from His hand. "Now stay here with Me and listen to My words. I have great plans for you, My girl."

"What kind of plans?" I ask.

"I will show you what you need to know as you need to know it." He says. "But I'm excited because you are starting to hear My voice and obey Me. Now I know that My plans for you can succeed, if only you continue to listen and trust and obey. Trust Me, Baby Girl. I will help you to obey Me. Obedience is so important."

Precious Daughter

"Lord, is there something You've told me that I still need to do, to obey?" I ask. "Show me."

"Don't worry about that right now," He says. "I am the one who searches the hearts, and I will show you what you need to know when you need to know it. Keep looking to Me and trusting Me. You know you can trust Me. Trust Me with your WHOLE HEART. It's good that you've been reading again. Fill your heart and mind with My words. I will instruct you and teach you in the way you should go. I will counsel and guide you with My eye upon you" (Psalm 32:8).

Let My Words Wash Over You

**Jesus is standing by the river, beckoning me to COME. I come to Him as a little child, about eight or nine years old. We walk together along the banks of the stream. He stoops and points to some rocks in the stream – the water rushes over them, making little white-water rapids. "See how the water is making those rocks smooth?" Jesus asks. I see that they still have some roughness to them, but they are mostly smooth. "Over time, the water of My word makes you smooth," He says.

"David chose five smooth stones," I say, "and You used one of them to knock down the giant. And then David was able to use the giant's own sword to kill him."

"Yes," Jesus says, "let My words wash over you. As you read and meditate on My words, they will make you fit for My use, as a smooth stone. I have prepared things for you that you have never thought of before. No one has ever seen or heard or thought of the things I have for you personally, Patty. Get ready. I am about to reveal things to you. Don't try to figure it out. Come to me as a child. A child doesn't assume to know, but seeks to learn. "

Precious Daughter

"How do I get ready, Lord?" I ask.

"I already told you. Be like a little child, ready to learn. Do you remember your excitement to start school when you were five years old and how you loved to go? Be like that. You got up early, got dressed and waited. Have that same joyful anticipation."

I look up at the trees that arch over us (in my vision), like a cathedral. I sing in tongues in worship, and I think Jesus is singing with me.

(Note: On my first day of kindergarten, I woke up long before everyone else in my house and got dressed. I remember being excited to wear my new outfit which had been laid out the night before. I was so excited to start school like my big sister who was four grades ahead of me in school.)

Chapter 10

The Tabernacle

Jesus Takes Me In

Exodus 40 The tabernacle…

"Oh Father," I pray, "bring me in. Jesus will take me into the Holy of Holies. Today I read about the tabernacle, but also about Jesus on the cross, how the veil was torn, and the soldiers said 'Surely this was the Son of God!' "

** Jesus takes me by the hand, walking me through the tabernacle.

Hebrews 10:19-22

By the brazen altar: I remember Jesus on the cross, and He says, "It is finished!"

By the brazen laver: He dips with His hands into the water and pours it on my hands. "You can come near with clean hands and a pure heart," He says.

I ask, "My hands are clean, but what about my heart?"

Then Jesus embraces me, and His love goes into my heart. "My love cleanses your heart. Be filled with it till there's room for nothing else."

The Tabernacle

Jesus takes me by the hand, and we go into the **holy place.** We can see the **golden candlestick** to the left. The golden walls reflect the light, and it's quiet and beautiful. He brings me to the **table of showbread**, and asks, "What about your will? Will you obey Me? Will you surrender your own will completely?"

"I want to, Lord," I reply, "but I don't know if I can. I think I need for my will to be ground fine like flour so I can offer it."

Jesus says, "I'm working on that, but all I need from you right now is your decision to surrender your will to me."

"Yes, absolutely," I say.

Jesus picks up my piece of bread and eats a bite. He smiles and says, "Tastes good."

We walk over to the **candlestick.** "Here, My Holy Spirit anointing burns and gives light to the inside of your soul," Jesus says. "I shine and light up any dark places in your soul, and My light causes the darkness to flee."

"Is there darkness?" I ask. "Search me, O God, and know my heart: try me and know my thoughts: and see if there be some wicked way in me, and lead me in the everlasting way" (Psalm 139:23-24).

I see a couple things and confess them, but Jesus says not to write them down, because once the light shines on them, the darkness is gone. He cleanses me from all unrighteousness.

Jesus says, "Inside, you are like this place, all glorious within. My Holy Spirit anointing lights you inside, and My presence is like the golden walls. The angels look in from heaven and rejoice at the light that they see. You shine like pure gold."

The Tabernacle

Now we walk over to the **altar of incense**. "What do you want to talk about?" Jesus asks.

I tell Jesus about all the people that I care about and am concerned for.

"OK," Jesus says, "let's lay these things on this altar and burn them. That means you give them to Me and to My Father, and let the smoke rise to heaven. You can say, 'Let Your kingdom come: let Your will be done on earth, as it is in heaven.'"

"Yes, Lord," I say. As other people come to my mind, I mention them by name. "I ask You to bless them."

Let's Go In Now

Jesus says, "Let's go in now; you see the veil is torn." We step into the **Holy of Holies. There is a powerful light here that fills the whole room. I can only worship the Father here. "Holy, Holy, Holy," I say in hushed tones. There's a powerful feeling of awe, making it hard to stand. Jesus holds my hand, so I don't fall down. "Father, Spirit, Son, I worship You. The glory is here."

Jesus says, "I've showed you the way. You can come in here every day. Now, is there anything you want to ask?"

"I need wisdom," I reply. "Speak to my spirit; I'm listening."

"Sweet Baby Girl," Jesus says, "rest in My presence. Stay in My presence. I love to have you come close. I love you. Let me fill your heart. Give Me your heart. I will form it and change it and make it new each day. I make all things new. I have been leading you, and you are at this moment in the center of My will. I brought you here, so I can speak to you face to face."

The Tabernacle

She's With Me

(Another day some weeks later, Jesus takes me through the tabernacle again.)

At the gate – No one could come in without a sacrifice. I offer myself, and Jesus is with me; the Lamb of God who takes away the sin of the world. "She's with Me," He says, and we pass through the **gate.

I think about what I've been reading, how they used the blood to cleanse the leper, anointing his right ear, right thumb, and right big toe. Some blood was brought in and put on the horns of the **altar of incense**, and then some was sprinkled on the priest. The rest was poured out at the base of the **altar.** Blood was on the doorposts at Passover. When Jesus' blood was shed at the cross, He said, "It is finished."

"Yes," Jesus says, "My blood is enough to take away the sins of the world. Your prayers must be under the blood as well."

We walk to the **laver**. Jesus says, "My word washes you, and you are clean. You drink My words by My Spirit, and your heart is clean." Jesus gives me water to wash with and then water to drink.

The mirrored surface of the laver reminds me, and I ask Him to search me. I confess some sins to Him, but I'm not to write them down. "You are cleansed from ALL unrighteousness," He says.

He holds His hand out to me and says, "Let's go in." Jesus pulls aside the curtain, and we step in. It's hushed and still and peaceful. Jesus and I are the only ones inside. We step over to the **table of showbread**. "Your will needs to be offered up fresh every day."

The Tabernacle

"Yes, Lord," I say, and I put my freshly baked cake of bread on the table. "Let Your kingdom come, and Your will be done."

We walk over to the **lamp stand**; "Notice, it's all one piece of gold but with seven lights, seven aspects of My Spirit," Jesus says, "the Spirit of the Lord, wisdom and understanding, counsel and strength, knowledge and fear of the Lord (Isaiah 11:2). Keep My lamp lit in your heart. The inner light is more important than the outer light. My Spirit gives you light from within."

Jesus takes my hand and brings me to the **altar of incense**. "You carry the names of My people on your heart," Jesus tells me, "just like the high priest had the names of My people on his breastplate, the names of the 12 tribes."

I pray for the people that are on my heart.

We step into the **Holy of Holies**. "I'm glad you've come," Father says. "You belong here. You are My daughter. I love you. Stay a few more minutes. Stay close to Me today. Be aware of My presence. Walk by faith."

More Oil *(another day)*

In my vision, I'm at the **brazen laver with Jesus, outside the tabernacle in the wilderness. "Search me, oh God, and know my heart: try me and know my thoughts," I say. "There's still some idolatry with food. If I was in the desert eating only manna like the Israelites, I would not be content either. Lord, please help me to surrender food and eating to you. I take authority over the spirit of gluttony in Jesus' name. I cast it away from me. I confess and repent of my participation with the spirit of gluttony. I confess and REPENT.

The Tabernacle

I ask You Father, for more of Your love that will cast out the fear of being hungry."

God answers, "My love is all you need, and more. My love fills you. You confessed your sin, and I cleanse you from all unrighteousness. I forgive you. This cleansing doesn't depend on you, but on Me. "

"Let's go in now," Jesus says. We step into the tabernacle, the **holy place.** There's a hushed reverence here. At the **table of showbread** I say, "I offer my will to You. I want to love You with all my heart, soul, mind and strength." I place a little flat bread on top of the stack; it represents my will.

Jesus pats it and says, "Good."

We walk over to the **lamp stand**. "Is there enough oil in my lamp? Do the wicks need trimming?"

Jesus replies, "You can ask Me for more."

"Please give me more, Lord," I ask. "Would You give me more oil and more anointing?"

Jesus takes a decanter and pours golden oil into each bowl of the **lamp stand**. "Wisdom, understanding, knowledge and fear of the Lord, counsel and strength, the Spirit of the Lord," He says as He fills each one (Isaiah 11:2). Then He takes scissors and trims the wicks. The lamps are burning bright and clean, reflecting off the golden walls. "Now your light will burn brightly all day. This represents the light in your heart, soul and spirit. You need to keep filled so your lamps don't go out."

Now we step over to the **altar of incense**. "What's on your heart? Who's on your heart?" Jesus asks.

The Tabernacle

I look down at my chest; the breastplate is there with rows of precious stones. I tell Him the names of the people I care about. I spend time talking to Jesus about those I have in my heart.

Holy of Holies

"I'm with you, always and forever. Come into My throne room. I have something for you." Jesus takes me by the hand. We go into the **Holy of Holies.** I see the **ark**, the **mercy seat**, the **angels**, and the glory cloud. Jesus puts His arm around me. "What do you want? What's your heart's desire? Ask."

"I want my sons to walk with You. I want David to grow into the man You want him to be, to fulfill Your purpose for his life and to be healed. And I want to be set free from the spirit of gluttony."

"All you need to be set free has been done," Jesus says. "Take the authority I have given you over the spirit of gluttony. I set you free, and you are free indeed. Now, you only need to walk out your freedom. Confess this as sin when it raises its ugly head."

You Need Fresh Oil *(some weeks later)*

I'm a little disappointed, because I haven't been hearing or receiving new words or visions lately. I don't look forward to journaling as I did before.

"Forget the former things; don't dwell in the past. See, I do new things," God answers. "My love for you is new every morning, and you need fresh oil. Even now I pour out My oil, My anointing of My Spirit on you. Get ready. You need Me, and you need FRESH OIL! I have been speaking to you in the night watches. Ask Me when you don't know what to do and even when think you do know what to do. Open your heart to receive from Me; open your spiritual ears to

The Tabernacle

listen. You can still hear My voice; only you haven't been taking the time to journal what you are hearing. I want to wash away that disappointment from you. You need to forgive yourself. I can work this together for good for you. Give it to Me, Baby Girl."

Chapter 11

Following Jesus Into the Battle

The Work of the Ministry is Mine

(I received this word for our Mexico Healing Rooms' directors, Jesús and Diana. We were in the car on the way to their house for our weekly meeting. We were discouraged, because only one person showed up for our new training class the week before.)

"Fix your eyes on Me," says the Lord, "Don't look at the circumstances, nor at any other person besides Me. The work of this ministry is Mine. Fix your eyes on Me. Call to Me. Ask Me for more laborers for the harvest. There is land that the enemy has in his hands, but I'm sending you to conquer this land. This is the time to proclaim freedom, everything in Isaiah 61. I have many people in this city, but they need to hear about My purpose for their lives. Many believers are bound by sickness. From the same people that come to receive healing, some are called to form teams of co-laborers. Pay attention; look at the ones that I have healed and are being healed. I will show you which ones have this calling. Pray to Me for more laborers for My harvest; ask the team to pray as well."

*(Later as we were praying together, I saw a vision. Note: This was the start of a **major continuing vision** that I came back to over the next days, weeks and months, and God revealed more each time. In fact, He is still revealing more to me as days go by. I am including all the*

Following Jesus into Battle

parts together here for continuity sake, and then will come back to other entries in my journal.)

Following Jesus into the Battle

** The Lord Jesus is mounted on a white horse, ready for battle. He is dressed in royal clothes, but also ready for battle, with sword and shield and royal helmet and breastplate, etc. He turns back to look at us, and on His face is a big smile. He makes a motion with His hand for us to follow Him into battle. There are horses for us as well, and quickly about 20 of us mount them. Now Jesus' smile gets bigger. We know we can be confident in the battle, because He goes before us.

(The next day I received this explanation of the vision.)

"You have absolutely no need to fear," Jesus says. "I don't just send you out into battle; I call you to come with Me and fight. I am your salvation. I give you authority to overcome over ALL the power of the enemy; with Me, by My Spirit. Not by might nor by power, but by My Spirit (Zech. 4:7). My Spirit is with you and in you. Depend on Me; depend on My Spirit for all that you do."

"I'm rejoicing and happy because I know if you follow Me into battle, the victory is ours," Jesus tells me. "It's when you go your own way, trying to fight on your own, or avoiding the battle completely, that you suffer defeat. Follow Me. Following Me is simple! Just fix your eyes on Me, and go where I lead you."

Royal Warriors

**Jesus gallops into battle. His horse is in front of mine, and there are other saints on horses in a line following Him to my right and left. We are all royal warriors. We have armor and weapons but also royal garments. For example, I see myself as a princess going into battle,

Following Jesus into Battle

dressed beautifully. My horse is a light chestnut color. My helmet is also a crown; I have a golden breastplate and belt, and a velvet jacket of red and rose. I'm wearing a long dress of rose and gold brocade, but its fabric is sturdy, and it has a split skirt so I can ride. I'm wearing sturdy boots of light brown. I have a bronze shield on my left arm, and I'm holding a bow in my right hand, and a quiver of arrows hangs from my waist alongside my thigh. "The arrows represent truth," Jesus says. "Follow me, and I will teach you how to shoot arrows of truth straight and true, right to the mark" (Psalm 18:34). "David knew the secret of trusting Me in the battle," Jesus says. He smiles as only He can, and we gallop into battle.

This Is My Land

**Jesus flashes another smile at all of us, then raises His sword and picks up the pace. We're advancing to the top of a hill or small mountain where there are dark, oppressive enemy clouds. But Jesus goes ahead, and the clouds dissipate before Him. The demon forces on the ground are sent running down the other side of the mountain. At the top of the hill, He circles with His horse and then reaches down with His sword and plants it firmly in the ground as He dismounts. "This is My land; I claim it for the Kingdom!" He shouts. On hearing this, the enemy hoard that had held the land retreats, cowering further down the other side of the mountain with the oppressive black cloud following them.

We all dismount from our horses, and Jesus directs us to join hands in a circle. Jesus steps to the center of the circle where His sword is. "My word of truth and My presence cause the enemy to flee, but I would not have come here and gained this ground unless you all had followed Me." There are about 20 of us princes and princesses in the circle around Jesus who says, "We will hold this ground with the truth." Each of us takes our arrows and swords and plants them in the ground in the circle next to us. "My words of truth will quickly take back the land. My truth will hold it. You are the leaders. Others will come and stand on this ground to occupy it, but they are weaker and will need to hear and see that you follow Me, that you stand for the truth and are willing to fight for it. The enemy has conceded this territory, but he lurks close by and will be seeking opportunity to wound and destroy the people who follow you here. Watch and pray. Keep looking to Me, and stand guard, and this territory will stay in My kingdom."

The mountain we have conquered is bleak and barren; nothing but dry, dusty dirt and rocks is all we can see for miles. We look around, and we can see the enemy in little camps all around the mountain. Some of us raise our swords, and they shine and cause the enemies to retreat further away.

"Be careful to keep your eyes on Me," Jesus says. We all turn back to look at Jesus, and then I see that the enemies behind Jesus down the hill retreat even further. The same happens on all sides as we look to Jesus. I know there was a danger in getting our eyes off of Jesus and onto ourselves.

Sending Some Out

**"Now I'm sending some of you out to bring more people here," Jesus announces. So He chooses two people to go one way and two to go another way. Before they go, Jesus checks their armor and their weapons, personally touching each article, adjusting a helmet here, tightening a buckle there. He gives each of them a larger shield, and they mount their horses. We can all see the direction they are going; they must pass the enemies closely on both sides and go under the dark clouds of oppression to get to their destination. "I am

Following Jesus into Battle

with you always even when you don't see Me," Jesus says. "I am a shield to you on the right hand and the left. He positions their shields so that one carries it on the right and the other on the left of the pair of horses. Then He slaps the horses to send them off quickly.

Jesus steps back into the circle, and we all stand at attention, looking to Him. As Jesus speaks to us, He keeps personal eye contact with each of us, so it seems He is always facing me, talking to me directly, and I know the same is happening to each of us in the circle. "Your job is to watch and pray and hold this ground. Soon more people will come but only if you pray to My Father, the Lord of the harvest, to send more laborers into His harvest." At this word, we all fall to our knees, and leaning on our swords and arrows, our shields upright by our sides, we begin to pray. We pray for more laborers; we pray for our coworkers who were sent out, that God would give them words to convince others to come with them.

Taking More Ground

**Jesus smiles, "Now we need to take more ground." Jesus teaches me how to shoot my arrows of truth, and then He points to a place about a half mile away where the enemy is lurking. I take up an arrow; I know it's an arrow of truth, but I want to know which truth I am sending out. "Trust in the Lord," Jesus says. So I shoot the arrow of − 'Trust in the Lord' − and it lands point down into the ground close to the enemy camp and causes them to retreat further away. I know that the enemy will not dare come near that arrow and that the ground around it now belongs to the kingdom. Jesus does the same with all the others, teaching some of them how to shoot arrows and others how to use their swords.

Now Jesus sends two men out to prepare the way for the people who are coming. Again, before they go, He checks their swords and

Following Jesus into Battle

each piece of armor and gives them larger shields, placing them to the right and to the left. These are going out on foot. He shows them how to hold their swords high with both hands and the swords shine brightly with a light of their own. He says, "I send out My light and My truth; let them lead you."

We watch them go in the direction that one of the pairs on horses went. As they pass between the enemy camps, the enemy retreats on both sides, widening the path. "I am the Light of the world. He who follows Me will not walk in darkness but will have the light of life," Jesus says (John 8:12). The dark clouds of oppression that partially covered the path also retreat way back. The two men walk for miles, having the same results; the enemy retreats wherever they go. Jesus sends two more in the other direction, two young women, with the same effect. The rest of us pray for these royal warriors, watching over them till they return.

Interpretation

I asked God for interpretation of what I received so far. Here's what I feel He answers, "The mountain that we took does not represent a specific place. The reason you could not recognize any of the royal warriors is because they represent all of My church leaders, not specific people. The mountain represents physical places and also spiritual areas of My church that the enemy has held in darkness for years. That's why you see nothing green growing on the mountain. The message of this vision is to be shared with leaders and pastors. This vision is not for you alone or for any one ministry. I entrusted it to you so that you would share it."

"Here's how it relates to healing ministry, not just in Mexico, but worldwide. The mountain represents an area of people's lives where the devil has taken over. My people don't trust me for their own healing, much less for others. This is why the arrow of truth – 'Trust in the Lord' – is so important. Once My people inhabit this ground again, the ground will begin to produce. My light and truth will take back the land quickly, but holding the land and keeping the enemy away will take time and will require more of My people."

Back to the vision: **Those of us who are with Jesus on the mountain have pushed back the enemy so that his camps are distant, about two miles away instead of a half mile, but the ground is still dry, dusty and barren and nothing is growing there. We can see there are clear pathways for the people who will soon be joining us.

Pray For Rain

**Pray for rain," Jesus says. We all kneel again with our swords and arrows planted in the land as we pray for rain. Beautiful, white cumulus clouds start forming on one side of the mountain where one of the paths is. We can see it start to rain there. It rains hard, and the clouds move on all around the mountain. Wherever it rains, it starts to get green as grass grows right away. We had shot out many arrows that are now planted in the ground all around the mountain. Wherever there is an arrow of truth, in that spot flowers, plants and even trees come up like a beautiful yard or garden.

After raining all around the mountain, finally it rains on us on the top of the mountain. It rains hard, but it is very refreshing for all of us. The grass grows under our feet, and the circle we stand in is quickly surrounded by flowering trees and bushes.

The mountain and the surrounding area are completely transformed. The dark clouds of the enemy camps seem farther away now. Maybe they retreated even further during the rain, or maybe it only seems like it because of the beauty around us. There is now a beautiful stream flowing out of the ground from the spot where Jesus' sword is planted. It flows meandering down one side of the mountain and then follows alongside one of the paths for as far as we can see into the valley below.

These People are Ready to Work

** As we are gazing at this stream, we can see a group coming up that same path. As they come closer, we recognize the pair of royal warriors that Jesus had sent out in that direction with a group of 20 or 30 people following them. Some are carrying tools, and others carry boards.

Jesus smiles and says, "These people are ready to work." I look at the followers who have come and see that they are dressed in ordinary, casual and work clothes. They all come up to the top of the mountain to see Jesus, rejoicing at how green and beautiful it is. We all rejoice with them and tell them how it happened.

Jesus gives them each a welcoming hug and then leads them down the hill to show them where the first building will be, next to one of the gardens that sprang up where an arrow had landed. Jesus shows them how to dig down to the bedrock and how to use the rocks and stones that are all around the area to make a foundation and walls for the house. The stones appear to be the same kind of volcanic rock that's typical of the area where we live here in Mexico. Jesus says, "A wise man builds his house on the rock. You are wise if you hear My words and do them."

Some of us are assigned as watchers on the top of the hill, but we can see the progress of the building, and Jesus comes up from time to time to encourage us that we are where we should be.

Following Jesus into Battle

Jesus brings another team together to work with the wood, making furniture, doors, and window frames for the house. It's such a pleasure to watch Jesus personally directing this work and swinging a hammer with the others.

Unless the Lord builds the house, they labor in vain who build it. Unless the Lord guards the city, the watchman keeps awake in vain (Ps 127:1).

Watch and Pray

**I watch Jesus work with the wood down the mountain a ways. Jesus comes up the hill again to talk to us. There are about six of us who are to guard the mountain, watching and praying. "Watch and pray, and we will keep this mountain," Jesus says. "More people will come here and learn to trust Me."

Now He talks to me personally, "Patty, I love you. You have been patient to wait on Me and look to Me. You can hear My voice, because My Spirit is in you. I have works prepared for you that you can walk in them. Soon you are going back to Minnesota, but spiritually you will still be on this mountain, teaching people to trust in Me. Trust in Me with all your heart. Don't lean on your own understanding. Look to Me wherever you go, and I will lead you on the right path (Prov. 3:5-7). Make certain you build according to My plans, that you are not building according to your own plans. Keep your focus on Me, and see what I'm doing. I have a plan for you. You are to be an intercessor, a watcher on the wall or mountain."

Now he speaks to all of us watchers, "Yes, I have a plan for building, but you are called to watch and pray. You are those whose job it is to stay on the mountaintop and pray and watch. From this place I show you things that others need to know. The renewal of the land was as a result of prayer. The rains would not have come if you hadn't prayed. I call you to pray. Therefore, you have to be in a place set apart, so you can hear My voice and I can teach you how to pray."

Pray for More Laborers

**"Pray for more laborers. The other team I sent out has not yet returned," He says. "Pray for their safety. They are on their way back here with a group of people, but the people are weak and are making slow progress. Pray for them that they will keep following their leaders. Some of them are listening to the enemy and are wounded. They need to put on the whole armor that I have provided. They need encouragement, and their leaders also need encouragement. They know they need to come here. The leaders remember that I sent them, but they have forgotten that I am with them even when they don't see Me. The dark clouds of enemy oppression are covering them, and they can't see the path very clearly either. Pray for them! They still have many miles to go. They haven't yet arrived to the clear path."

We kneel down and lean on our swords again. Jesus has put this burden on us to pray, about six of us, and four are new ones who came with the group that recently arrived. They have swords and shields but small ones.

Leaning on my sword, I lead out in prayer. "Father, open the eyes of our fellow workers who are coming here. Help them to see that Jesus really is with them. I pray that their leaders would use their swords and shields to fight off the lying spirits. I pray that You would send them strong encouragement, so they would know that You, God, are for them. Then who can be against them? Help the new ones to put on their whole armor that You have provided." As I pray, I find myself wishing that my sword would be bigger, that I would have a better

Following Jesus into Battle

knowledge of the word of God. I know my prayer is only effective if I lean on my sword (the word of God), and it's not very big; the blade is about a foot and a half long. The swords of the new intercessors are even smaller, about the size of a kitchen knife with blades about eight to ten inches long, kind of hard to lean on. But they do lean on them as they pray. I pray, "Lord grant us a spirit of wisdom and revelation in the knowledge of You and Your word."

I continue to pray, searching my heart for scripture that applies to the situation. *(Note: I know that this prayer is important for what is happening today, the situations only represented by my vision. I invite other intercessors reading this to pray with me now...)* "Lord, give Your angels charge concerning them to keep them in all their ways. Let them trust You. You are a shield to all who take refuge in You. If they can trust You with all their heart, You will direct their path. We take authority over the enemy for their sakes, Father, with the authority that Jesus gave us to overcome all the power of the enemy. So we command the evil spirits to get away from them. Get far back from their path, in Jesus' name. Lord, help them to see the light again. God, You are light, and in You is no darkness at all.

"Lord, You heal the brokenhearted and bind up their wounds. Heal those in the group who have been wounded by the enemy. Help the group to see that their leaders really are on the right path. Oh, LORD, open their eyes that they may behold wondrous things in Your word."

I Want to Make You Fruitful *(About two months later)*

**"Ask Me," Jesus says. "Keep asking Me when you don't know what to do. I'll help you and show you. I love you, Baby Girl. Be careful not to assume you know what to do. Ask Me. I will help you and show you the way to go. Cast your burden on Me, all your burdens."

Following Jesus into Battle

Jesus is by the stream. He takes my hand and leads me to the top of the little mountain where my group is praying. "I want to make you fruitful. You will bear fruit for Me, Precious One." Some of the trees around our prayer circle are bearing fruit. Some of the workers from down the hill who are building come up and pick the fruit for a snack, and then they drink from the stream that flows from the ground where Jesus' sword was planted. Jesus tells us intercessors, "Keep watching and praying. Your prayers bear fruit."

(Another two months have past.) I was working at Healing Rooms last night, when another Healing Rooms volunteer spoke these words over me, "You are a mighty woman of God, known in heaven and on earth and wherever you go."

Today, Father says, "It's true, you are a princess, a royal warrior. Demons flee and cower in the corners to see what you will do and say. Your source of power and might is in Me and the authority I have given you. It is in trusting and resting in Me."

Jesus Teaches Me to Use My Sword

**I stand on the mountain before Jesus in my royal warrior clothes. Jesus is checking my armor. He adjusts my helmet and tightens straps on my breastplate and belt. Then He checks my bow. He takes my sword out of its sheath, and checks the edges for sharpness. He sharpens it more by wetting His fingers on His tongue, running them along the blade, then rubbing the blade on a thick leather strap He has attached to His belt. He sharpens both sides of the blade and the tip. He says, "The words you hear in the Spirit will sharpen and lengthen your sword."

I notice my sword is longer and sharper now, just what I had prayed for earlier. He hands it back to me, placing it in my two hands and

Following Jesus into Battle

then lifting my hands high. As it's lifted up, the sword shines and reflects the light, perfectly polished and beautiful, silver and gold, a royal sword.

"You see how sharp your sword is. There's a reason I have likened My word to a sharp sword. You must learn how to use it to be effective. Not by might, nor by power, but by My Spirit. As you tune in to My Spirit, you will be able to handle the sword of the Spirit which is My word. Be careful to use My words as an offensive weapon only against the enemy. With people, you can use My word against the oppression around them; you can use it to cut off the chains that bind them, but never use it against people. Hold up My sword as a light to them, as you are doing now. As they see the light, enemy oppression will loosen its grip on their hearts and minds. As they learn to use their own swords, these enemies will flee from them.

"There is much POWER in My word as it is directed by My Spirit. My word is living and active and sharper than any two-edged sword and piercing as far as the division of soul and spirit... Let My word do its work in you. When you hear My voice, do not harden your heart. The sword I have given you is long and sharp, and you are learning to use it. Learn to lean on it as you pray. Rest in Me. Trust Me even when My words cut you sharply. Do not harden your heart, and you will enter into My rest. Rest from your own works."

Now Jesus stands behind me and places His hands over my hands on the sword. He teaches me how to move my sword, slashing, raising it, and striking the rocks around us. My sword is big and heavy; it takes my two hands just to hold it up and Jesus' strength to make it move. I wonder how I can ever use the sword on my own with only one hand and the other hand holding my shield of faith.

Following Jesus into Battle

"I'm teaching you," Jesus answers. "Now you will have more respect for My word as a powerful weapon, being careful how you use it. I am the One who girds you with strength. Your strength is in Me. On your own, you can never handle this sword. My right hand upholds you, and My gentleness makes you great. Never try to use this sword as an offensive weapon unless My hands are on yours. You need My strength and skill. You can never use it on our own. Without Me, you can do nothing. Rest in Me and My words, and all things are possible. I have given you the shield of My salvation, and My right hand upholds you."

Now Jesus puts my shield on my left arm, still helping me to hold the sword with His right hand over my right hand. We swing the sword again, going through the same motions as before. Jesus says, "You never need to use this sword on your own, nor should you ever try. Never forget that I am with you to help you."

Mount Victory *(Several months later)*

"Lord," I ask, "is there more You want to show me about the sword vision or about the mountain?"

"Wait on Me to gird you with strength and make your way blameless," Jesus answers. "I can make your feet swift and sure and set you on high places. In your vision I brought you to the mountain. I also cinched your belt. I gird you with My strength (Psalm 18:32-33). When I touch you, My strength goes in to you. In the Spirit I am training you so you can wield the sword of the Spirit. If I bring you into a battle, I go before you. In your vision I showed you exactly where to shoot your arrows of truth. The hill we conquered is a place where My presence can be seen and felt. There is never a moment when you are unable to look to Me. You can call Me at any moment, and I am with you. Those who are sent out have My armor, and I am

113

Following Jesus into Battle

with them, but they don't often see or feel Me. They go by faith. You and the other intercessors are on the conquered mountain. Your job is to help them in prayer."

"Lord," I ask, "does the mountain have a name?"

"Victory," Father answers. "My right hand and My holy arm have gained the victory for me (Psalm 98:1). Jesus is My right hand and My holy arm. I send Him to gain victory through the Holy Spirit."

The horse is prepared for the battle, but the victory belongs to the Lord (Prov. 21:31).

"Lord," I ask, "what about the horses? Spiritually, what do they represent?"

"They represent My strength and the might and power of My Spirit," Jesus answers. "Worldwide change can only come when you follow Me by My Spirit. My leaders will ride fast and hard to follow Me. In these last days, I will rout out the enemy in many places and bring fruitfulness VERY QUICKLY, even as the rains you prayed for watered the barren land, and quickly there were mature plants and trees. I pour My Spirit out and quickly reverse the devastation and barrenness that the enemy has caused."

> 1Cor.15:54,57-58: Death is swallowed up in victory... Thanks be to God who gives us the victory through our Lord Jesus Christ. Therefore my beloved brethren, be steadfast, immovable, always abounding in the work of the Lord, knowing that your toil is not in vain in the Lord.

Following Jesus into Battle

You Are Doing an Important Work

**I'm in the circle on the mountain, my royal armor in place. I'm kneeling in the grass, and my sword is in the ground so I can lean on it. The stream flows from the place where Jesus' sword was planted. More workers have arrived and are helping with the building below. My companions, who are praying with me in the circle, have grown in strength, and their armor is more substantial. Their swords are longer, and their shields are bigger. Jesus comes up from the building to touch each one of us and encourage us. "Watch and pray," He says. "You are doing an important work."

"In the Spirit you can lean on the sword in prayer," He says. "Use the sword of the Spirit, which is the word of God, with all prayer and petition. Pray at all times in the Spirit, and with this in view, be on the alert with all perseverance and petition for all the saints (Eph. 6:18).

"I have caused your sword to grow by the words of My mouth," He says. "Now you can stand, leaning on your sword. Stand in prayer and hold the ground I have given to you. Watch and pray. Be on your guard and listen for My word to you. Praying in the Spirit includes listening. You are My child, Mine. Don't look at others and the way I have led them. Listen to Me; look to Me, and trust that I am leading and guiding you."

Praising Father on the Mountain

"I call you to be a watcher on the mountain," Jesus says. "I have taught you how to use your sword as an offensive weapon, making sure your hand is in Mine when you use it. Keep your sword polished and sharp by listening to My words and leaning on them in prayer. I

Following Jesus into Battle

..ave not withdrawn My calling for you. In fact, I want to re-affirm this calling today."

**I'm on the mountain, on my knees, leaning on my sword. I'm with the group of six of us, four of whom are new, and they now have shields and armor. We have all matured. Our swords are all longer and sharper. We all stand at once, and raise our hands to the God of heaven and earth, our swords and shields still planted in the earth. We sing in heavenly languages. Jesus comes and joins us and sings with us, and now I see angels also behind each one of us, two or three behind each one. Our little group is now a big company. The angels are singing with us. A few of the angels have instruments. The sound we make is so beautiful and heavenly.

Many of the workers come up from below to join us. We're still standing in a circle, but now the circle is five to seven deep, people and angels, all singing praise to God. Jesus steps to the center where the beginning of the stream is. He continues to praise the Father, His arms uplifted. The rest of us begin to quiet our voices, but He sings louder and motions for us to do the same. Now we're all singing loudly, "Holy, holy, holy!" There must be more than 100 voices all singing "Holy, holy, holy!" as loud as we can. Very powerful! The glory cloud comes down in a circular motion from heaven, counter clockwise as we continue to sing and shout "Holy!" It's like a sparkling mist with stars and brightness, and as it settles, each one of us shines or glows, Jesus most of all. Heaven has come to earth! Jesus' garments all shine brighter, and the people's garments are still colored, but they look like they're lit up, as with shimmering lights or jewels. We continue to sing "Holy, holy, holy" in awe and wonder. I notice our swords and shields are glowing and shining as well. There is such reverence and joy in the whole group.

Following Jesus into Battle

Jesus Comes to Each One

**Now we all sing in a heavenly language, in perfect harmony. We all sing the same words, and even though I don't understand exactly what we're singing, I know it's a song of thanks and praise. The song softens in volume until we're all singing quietly and sweetly. Jesus comes to each one of us believers and tells us the things we need to know about our own personal destiny, while everyone else sings softly and reverently. When He comes to each person, He puts His hands affectionately on either side of his or her face and stands very close speaking to them personally.

We're singing of the love of God, how sweet and precious, how rich and pure:

"We will sing of Your love, We will sing of Your love

Your love is forever, so rich and pure

Holy is Your love, God

Sweet, Your words of love

It's everything we need, God, and even more

Your love fills us; Your love moves us

It fills us with Your hope; It fills us with Your joy

It brings us peace

Your love is precious; Your love is beautiful

Your love is all we need and even more"

Following Jesus into Battle

Now It's My Turn

**Jesus has made His way around to me, and it's my turn. He cups my face in His two hands and says, "Patty, I am pleased with you. Precious One, Sweetness and Light, you are a princess in My kingdom. I love it that you come to Me every day. I love it that you long for more of My love and My Father's love. I have great plans for you. You will be surprised at what I can do with you and where My Spirit will take you. Keep on keeping on. Be sure to spend time watching and listening each day."

Your Prayer Causes Heavenly Actions

"Father," I ask, "what would You say to me? What would You have me do?"

"Trust in Me with your whole heart," God says. "Don't lean on your own understanding. Lean on Me. I'm with you. I will help you. I strengthen you, and you are strong in Me. You are a watcher on My mountain. I trust you to listen to My voice. Even when you don't take time to watch and pray, I'm faithful. I will be with you to help you. You are so precious to Me."

** I'm on the mountain, Mount Victory, with the other watchers. We're standing in a circle. Jesus is down the hill working on the house. The house is made of stone with wooden doors and window frames. The wooden roof is finished except for the shingles, and men are hammering down shingles of wood. Jesus is supervising and helping. Jesus is so young and strong. He climbs up the ladder onto the roof with grace and confidence. He encourages each worker. He comes down again and talks with a man who is cutting glass panes to fit in the windows. Then He strides up the hill to talk to us. "Your

Following Jesus into Battle

work here is important. You use your swords in prayer, and the enemy stays away from this mountain."

"Your prayers cause heavenly actions," Jesus says. "I send My angels to carry out My will. As you lean on your swords and pray from My word, it will accomplish all that I say or have said, all that is written and heard. Pray, leaning on My words, rhema and logos. My word which goes forth from My mouth <u>shall</u> <u>not</u> return to me empty. My word will accomplish My desire. My word will SUCCEED. As surely as rain and snow water the earth and cause growth and fruitfulness, My word causes growth and fruitfulness (Isaiah 55: 10-11). Use My word as you pray. Lean on your sword; lean on My word."

I pray through Psalm 139...

"Search me, O God, and know my heart. Try me and know my anxious thoughts; and see if there be any hurtful way in me, and lead me in the everlasting way" (Psalm 139:23-24).

Night Is Coming

**I'm on the hill; I feel an urgency to be ready for battle. I pick up my shield of faith and cinch my helmet on securely. I make sure my breastplate and belt are secure. My sword is at my side, still planted in the ground. It's long enough now that I can stand and lean on it as I pray. The others in the circle do the same.

"You're right," Jesus says. "You need to be ready. <u>Night</u> <u>is</u> <u>coming</u>. Darkness will cover the earth, and deep darkness will cover the peoples. But I will rise upon you, and My glory will appear upon you. Arise, shine, for your light has come. And My glory, the glory of the LORD has risen upon you" (Isaiah 60:1-2).

Following Jesus into Battle

"See," Jesus says, "I'm here with you, although all around this mountain enemy oppression reigns. You have come to My mountain, My holy hill. You are part of My kingdom. Look around you."

We are on top of the mountain made green and lush by the Lord's rain. There are many fruit trees and palm trees There are fields of crops and grains all around the mountain. The house just below us on the side of the mountain is almost finished. Everywhere I look on the mountain and next to the mountain, people are working, rejoicing, planting and harvesting, picking fruit and using the river water to irrigate fields.

But far off on all sides, I can see dark clouds of enemy oppression. I think about the people who live under that oppression. They can't even see that light, hope and fruitfulness exist.

Send Warriors to Fight

**"O Lord," I start to pray, and the others are also praying, "I pray that You send out Your light and Your truth. Send messengers to bring more people into Your light. You told us, 'You are the world's light.' Open people's eyes; remove the darkness of oppression so they can see the light that is so close. Lord, I'm torn; You've told me that I'm to stay and watch and pray, but I also want to go and tell them. So many people are in gross darkness. Send warriors to fight the enemy. Send preachers to preach the good news that people don't have to live in darkness. How then will they call on You in whom they have not believed? How will they believe in You if they haven't heard? And how will they hear without a preacher? How will they preach unless they're sent?"(Romans 10:14-15).

Jesus smiles broadly, "I've been waiting for you to pray this prayer!"

Following Jesus into Battle

Called and Chosen

**Jesus goes down the hill to the workers in different places. He taps several of them on the shoulder, and then I see Him pointing to the top of the hill where we are standing. One by one, several workers come up to the top of the hill and say, "Jesus sent us here." If these are the preachers Jesus is sending out, I'm thinking they aren't ready yet. They're dressed in work clothes ready for work, but they have no armor.

"Lord," I pray, "are these the ones? They aren't ready!"

Jesus comes up and tells us, "These are My called and chosen preachers. They are missionaries, but you're right, they aren't ready. That's why they haven't been sent out. They need intercessors to pray for them. They need mentors to disciple them."

We see that we can start by praying for them. Jesus gathers them into the center of our circle. There are maybe eight of them, and we lay hands on them and pray. Jesus has gone to the outside of our prayer circle, and He lays hands on us intercessors, not on the potential preachers. But we feel His strength and power going through us to them.

Lord, They Need Your Armor

"Lord," I pray, "they need Your armor."

Jesus answers, "I have armor prepared just for them, but they haven't felt the need to put it on yet. Since they arrived here, they have stayed near My mountain where there is light, fruitfulness, and faithfulness. Until now, they didn't even notice the oppression around them. Pray for their eyes to be opened."

Following Jesus into Battle

"Yes, Lord, open their eyes to the need all around us," we pray. "They have been obedient to Your calling by coming here. I know that You can do all things. You can prepare them quickly. You prepared Your disciples in three years; then the Father sent the Spirit to empower them. Lord, help us to see as well, to see what they need so we can pray for them. Cause them to grow in Your word, so they have swords to fight against the enemy. Appoint mentors to disciple them." As I pray, I have one hand on my sword, which is planted in the ground, and my other hand is laid on the backs of the workers closest to me, first one then another. The other intercessors do the same.

Now one of the workers, a strong young man, leads out in prayer, "Lord, there are so many people living in oppression. It is so dark there. I remember my family and my old friends. They need to come here to live in victory. I want to tell them, but I'm not ready. Make me ready, O God."

Jesus smiles and snaps His fingers, and an angel comes carrying a set of armor. He stands ready and waiting. The young man sees it and rejoices. "It's for you," Jesus says. The young man puts on the helmet of salvation; it's a perfect fit. It's a leather helmet with metal plates on it. We all watch as the young man puts on his breastplate, his belt of truth and his gospel boots. Jesus hands the shield to him and then the sword, they are both small, but we know they will grow as he puts his trust in God and learns His word. There is such a transformation in this young man as he receives his armor. His face brightens, and he looks more determined.

"These who stand here as watchers on My mountain will train you to use your shield and sword," Jesus says. "They have experience."

Following Jesus into Battle

I look to Jesus with a questioning look and remember that He Himself trained me.

"Of course, I'm always here to help as well," Jesus says. "I will supervise your training."

The young man's sword and shield are small, so he looks with respect at our swords and shields, which have grown so much over the years. "Your shield and sword will grow larger during your training," Jesus assures him.

The other workers ask Jesus for armor as well. Several angels are summoned and each brings a set of armor for one worker. "Put on the whole armor of God, so that you will be able to stand firm against the schemes of the devil," Jesus says.

Prayer for Armor of God *(This is a helpful prayer to pray based on Eph 6:10–18. I often write out prayers like this one that are based on scripture. In this way, I know my prayers have power. I'm using the word of God, the powerful sword of the spirit, in my prayers.)*

"Thank You, God, that I can be strong in You and in the power and strength of Your might, as I put on the FULL armor of God, the armor that comes from You. I put it on now, so that I may be able to stand FIRM against the schemes of the devil. My struggle is not against other people, or even against my own flesh, but against rulers and powers and world forces of this darkness, against spiritual forces of wickedness in the heavenly places. So I put on Your whole armor, God, so that I will be able to resist in the evil day and do everything and stand FIRM.

"I'm standing now, and truth is like a belt around my waist. I put on Jesus' righteousness as a breastplate to protect my heart from

Following Jesus into Battle

attack. My <u>feet</u> <u>are</u> <u>prepared</u> <u>to</u> <u>bring</u> <u>peace</u>, the good news of peace to people wherever I go. I take up the <u>shield</u> <u>of</u> <u>faith.</u> All things work together for good for me (Rom. 8:28), and with this shield I am able to quench ALL the fiery darts of the evil one. I take the <u>helmet</u> <u>of</u> <u>salvation</u>; I know that I'm saved, healed and delivered. My <u>sword</u> <u>of</u> <u>the</u> <u>Spirit</u> <u>is</u> <u>Your</u> <u>word,</u> God, and I'm ready to use it whenever the enemy attacks. I also pray now and at all times in the Spirit with this in view: I am on the alert with all perseverance and petition for all the saints. I pray on behalf of Your ministers, especially, that words be given as they open their mouths with boldness to speak of the mystery of the gospel. I pray all this in Jesus' name."

Chapter 12

Quiet Your Heart

With Jesus in the River

**I'm with Jesus in the river; we're hand-in-hand, and I'm about eight years old. The water is up to my thighs. We're walking upstream in the water. The city is far off, barely visible, but I know we're going towards it. "Keep holding My hand, Patty," Jesus says. "Keep walking with Me, and you will always be close to My river, even when we head into battle. My river flows through you."

My Daughter, My Princess, My Bride

"Beautiful One, I love you," Father says. "You are My daughter, My princess, My bride. You don't know how precious you are to Me. Precious One, I love it that you danced for Me yesterday. I love the times that you devote to Me. I want to fill you in these times so that you have something to give to others. My blessing flows through you.

Last night when you were restless, hot, tired, and feeling empty, you could have come to Me sooner. Ask Me when you don't know what to do. Don't you think I might have some good ideas? Be aware of your tendency to go astray and turn to your own way. But you know My voice, so follow Me. I set you as a watcher, an intercessor. I have called you to come apart unto Me, to stand for others who need prayer, who need a touch from Me. Pray for more laborers; pray for

125

the workers who have become discouraged or distracted. I send them to you."

Quiet Your Heart

"Listen," Holy Spirit says. "My voice is a gentle whisper, like the wind through the leaves on the trees. I'm always speaking, but you have to tune in to notice and to listen. Be still. Quiet your heart and your own thoughts. I'm here as surely as the wind in the trees. You can hear it and feel it. You can see its results. As the leaves and branches respond to My wind, you respond to Me. Let Me move you. As the tree is planted in the ground and reaches deep with its roots to drink water, so let your roots go deep into the soil of My love. You are like a little branch connected to My tree. Apart from My love, you cannot live. Abide in Me, and stay connected to Me and to My words."

You Need Me

"Rest in Me, Precious One," Father says. "I love you so very much. You are My very own child. You need Me much more than you realize. More than a two-year-old needs her mother. You are like a helpless infant; without Me you can do nothing. You can't go anywhere unless I carry you. Rest in Me. I desire that kind of closeness with you, as a mother with a newborn child. Look to Me for everything, for every need. Trust in Me completely. You remember the way your babies looked into your eyes and drank in your love. Look into My eyes; look full in My face. You need My embrace, My closeness and My touch in just this same way. I love you so much, Precious One."

Quiet Your Heart

Princess

"I love you, Precious One," Jesus says. "Draw near. Come as a little child."

**Jesus is sitting on a rock by a river, and I come to Him as a little child, about five years old. He hugs me close. "I love you, Princess," He says. He commands an angel who brings my princess outfit; white sparkly dress, blue robe, blue satin slippers, and crown. Jesus helps me put them on over my blue pants and t-shirt. "These clothes are not just pretend," Jesus says. "You are a princess, My Princess. I see you as you are and as you will be. Dance with Me, My Princess." I dance with Jesus in my vision at the same time as I'm dancing in my living room. I'm a little child and an adult at the same time.

I Want to See the City

"Time goes by so quickly," I say.

"Yes," God replies, "for you time goes quickly, but I am Lord over time. I do not dwell in time, and I am in you. In this way, you can be timeless, not limited by time and space."

"I don't know if I'm hearing You right, Lord." I say.

"In the Spirit, you are already seated with Me in heavenly places," He explains. "You have already stepped into eternity. Eternity is in your heart. Look not at the things which are seen, but at the things which are not seen, the eternal things. Change your focus. Look to My city, the heavenly Jerusalem; look to My river and My throne."

"Lord," I beg, "I want to see the city; I want to see Your throne."

"You have asked for this, My Child," He says. "It's a good thing to ask for. You will see it. Focus on the things I show you; focus on Jesus, the river, the battle, and the waterfall. The river you see comes from My throne and from My city. You have tasted of the waters of My Spirit that come from My throne. Draw near to Me in My river. Drink from My river."

I Am the Source

"Everything good is in Me. I am the source. You see all the plants and flowers; all this profusion of life that has sprung up over one summer. This life was all here in the winter, but hidden and dormant. Roots, seeds and bare branches are now turned into an extravagance of abundant life. Many people, even most people are like this – having potential for life and growth, but lying dormant or sleeping like a long winter."

Let My River Flow In Power

"I have loved you with an everlasting love," God says. "I always love you. My love for you is greater, deeper and wider than you can imagine. I love you. Come to Me."

**I come to Jesus by the river. I'm eight or nine years old. He stoops to hug me, then He takes my hand, and we start walking upstream. We're at a place in the river where it's rushing over large rocks. The river is wide and deep and powerful, kind of like Spokane falls with lots of rushing water.

"My Spirit is deeper, wider and more powerful than you can imagine," Jesus says. "You will receive power when the Holy Spirit has come upon you (Acts 1:8). Be filled with My Spirit; be filled like this rushing, powerful river. This river will flow out from you, from your innermost being will flow rivers of living water (John 7:38). You have been drinking from My river by hearing My words. When you do My words, the river flows.

"Whenever you do My will, the river flows. Let My river flow in POWER. Put My words into action; believe in Me; believe in the Father; believe in My Spirit. My river of My Spirit flows through you. My Spirit teaches you all things; He is in you, and by Him you hear My voice (John 14:17,26). Tune in to the river within you; tune in to My Spirit, and He will teach you."

My Heart is to Encourage You

I'm feeling discouraged and out of sorts, and I hear God saying to me, "Call to Me, and I will answer you, and I will tell you great and mighty things you do not know" (Jer. 33:3).

I say, "I call to You God, Daddy, Jesus, Holy Spirit!!"

God answers, "I don't want you to be discouraged or anxious in any way. I want to bless you. I want to pour out blessing on you. I love you very much. Look to Me, and I will bless you. My heart is to encourage you.

"Eye has not seen nor ear heard… your eyes have not seen, your ears have not heard, and you have never even thought of the things I have prepared for you, because I love you and you love Me.

"You are My child, My most precious one, and I love you more than you can imagine. So cast off discouragement. It does not come from Me. Any time you feel the least bit discouraged, cast it off. You have authority over evil spirits of discouragement. The enemy wants you to be discouraged, but I want to encourage and bless you. I am FOR you. I am your refuge, your hiding place, your strong deliverer, and I love you.

Quiet Your Heart

"Ask Me to help you, and I will. Ask Me to anoint you for the tasks you have to do, and I will. My blessing is on you. My Holy Spirit is within you. Be blessed; be happy. Don't be dismayed or anxious about ANYTHING. Just tell Me how you are feeling. Give all your cares and burdens to Me. I Am the answer. You are so precious to Me. Be encouraged."

Under the Trees

** Jesus and I are walking by the river. The river here is wide, like the St Croix River. We're holding hands. I'm a young woman, maybe 25 or 30. "Allow Me to lead you, Sweetness," He says. "You don't know where to go or what to do on your own. Let Me lead you." Jesus leads me to a path that goes into the woods. I feel insecure because it seems to lead away from the river. "Don't worry, Patty," Jesus says. "I'm with you, and I'm leading you."

So we walk into the woods. It's darker here. "Does this mean You are leading Me into a difficult time?" I ask.

"Sweetness, don't be anxious," Jesus assures me. "Just rest in Me. I am leading you, and I will tell you what you need to know, when you need to know it. I supply all your needs. I hold your hand and watch over you." The woods are peaceful and quiet, and the path is broad and easy to walk on, about as wide as a car, but of hard packed earth.

I ask, "What do You want to show me? What do You want me to know?"

"Look at the trees," Jesus says. "See how they tower over us? See how they meet over the path? They show strength and wisdom."

Quiet Your Heart

I look at the trees. They are tall and sturdy; their trunks are bigger than I could reach around with my two arms. Their large branches reach up and make an archway over the path – beautiful. Jesus says to me, "Remember I told you to walk with Me under the trees? Why did you stop?" *(I haven't been reading lately from the John G. Lake book. He is one of the strong Christians or "trees" that the Lord wants me to receive from. See pages 24-25)*

"I'm sorry, Lord," I reply.

"Go ahead and read, now," Jesus says. "Walk with Me under the trees and receive strength and wisdom."

Get Ready! The Best is Yet to Come

****I'm with Jesus on the same path as yesterday. *(See Under the Trees.)* He gives me a hug. "Lord, I'm thirsty for You," I say. Jesus leads me to a little stream hidden right next to the path; in fact, it appears to come from under the path where we are standing. I had been feeling insecure about being away from the river, but the stream was there all the time! I stoop down to dip my hand and drink.

"Drink your fill," Jesus says. "You are hungry, too, hungry for Me and My words." Jesus takes my hand and helps me up. "Wait on Me now. Be still." Jesus puts His hand on my head, then makes a wiping motion from temple to temple across my forehead. "I renew your mind. I wipe out the old corrupted thinking. You have My mind, an anointed mind. I love you so much, and I want to help you. My Spirit fills you."

Jesus places His hands on my shoulders and smiles at me. "Get ready," He says. "The best is yet to come."

Quiet Your Heart

Suddenly, a big white horse comes bounding up the path behind us! Jesus mounts the horse, then reaches down to me and lifts me up behind Him on the horse. "Hang on!" He exclaims. I quickly link my hands in front of His waist, and off we go! We're galloping down the path at a fast pace. I don't know where we're going, but I don't need to know; Jesus is in control. All I have to do is hang on.

Just Hang On!

"Today is a new day. I make all things new. I'm with you, Baby Girl. Wait now. Listen. Look to me."

**I'm on the horse with Jesus. "I'll take you where you need to go," He says. We're galloping very fast down the path under the trees. I don't know where we're going. I look at Jesus, and He turns and flashes me a big smile, His teeth so white against His black beard and mustache and olive skin. "Just hang on!" He says. It's so wonderful that I can hang on to Jesus, this closeness on the horse, my arms around His waist.

"Lord," I ask, "is there anything more You want me to know about this?"

"I know you feel out of control," Jesus answers, "but you can trust Me even when it's a wild, fast ride. Hang on to Me! Stay close to Me. Stay on My horse! I know you would like to know where we are going, but you need to be content that you are with Me. I'm leading this horse and taking you quickly to where you need to go."

(Note: Later I shared this vision above with my husband John, and he thought that since I am reading the John G. Lake book, Jesus is moving me along quicker.)

Quiet Your Heart

Take Time to Listen and Talk to Me

"This time you take with Me is the most important thing you do," Father says. "Take time to listen to Me. Call to Me, and I will answer you."

"Show me Your ways that I may know You!" I say. "I call to You. Father, speak to me please. I need You so much."

**I come before His throne and kneel down before Him and bow with my face to the ground. He says, "Get up and talk to Me, Princess; tell Me about all that concerns you."

So I stand and tell Him about my concerns... classes I will teach... speech contest... my job... my son's finances...

God says, "Come closer, Sweetness." I come and lean on Daddy's lap, and He puts His arm around me. (My tears are flowing now as God touches my heart.) "You forget how much I love you," He says.

I tell Him about more cares and concerns...my weight...stuffy nose and body aches... tiredness...

"Talk to Me about it," He says. "You need rest," He says, "Take some extra rest today. Ask Me what to do; I will help you."

**Now I am a little girl about seven years old. Jesus picks me up and lays me down on a soft comforter under the tree, a pillow under my head. He covers me and tucks me in. "Rest," He says. He stays right with me, sitting beside me under the tree, watching over me.

Under the Trees *(next day)*

Under the trees is a key image. I knew I should take my John G. Lake book with me and read it when I laid down for a nap yesterday, so I

Quiet Your Heart

did. I slept for about an hour, and then read for about an hour and a half. Lake's sermons are so very powerful. I think this is one of the ways Jesus will take me where He wants me to go very quickly. Resting helped me to feel better, and also my husband John prayed for me; my nose was much better, and the congestion cleared up. I was able to go to Healing Rooms and pray for people last night. Praise the Lord!

Chapter 13

There is More

Keep Asking for More

"I have more for you, much more than you are walking in right now," Father says. "I want to give to you the spirit of wisdom and revelation in the knowledge of Me. Ask Me for it. Then ask Me for more. There's always more to know about Me. The eyes of your understanding will be enlightened. You will know the hope of My calling for you. You will know the riches of My inheritance in you (Eph. 1:17-18). Keep asking for MORE. There is much more than what you have been asking for."

"Lord," I say, "I confess and repent of fear, stress, anxiety and lack of trust in You. I repent for thinking I need to take care of my dad. God, I know that You will care for him. I put him in Your hands and my mom, too. I ask You to show me what to do about Dad and Mom and when to do it. I cast off discouragement in Jesus' name."

(My mom and dad are having health problems, and I'm having a hard time letting the burden of their care go, especially since our plan is to soon leave Minnesota and spend six months in Mexico.)

Riches of the Glory

"Sit still, and listen to Me for a while. Be in tune with My Spirit today."

There is More

"Oh God of our Lord Jesus Christ, Father of Glory," I pray. "Give me a spirit of wisdom and revelation in the knowledge of You. O, that the eyes of my heart may be enlightened so that I might know the hope of Your calling. I pray that I might know the riches of the glory of Your inheritance in the saints (in us). I ask that I may know the surpassing glory of Your power toward us (and toward me) who believe" (Eph. 1:17-19). "Show me Your ways that I may know You!"

**I'm in the river at a place where the water flows over some big rocks, like a small waterfall. I'm sitting in the water, and it's washing over me, over my head and my whole body. I feel like the water is gentle and warm and comforting.

River of My Delights

"I'm right here, and I love you," God says. "Be still, and listen to Me for a while. I want to bless you. I am your refuge. Hide away with Me for a little while. Drink your fill from the abundance of My house, from the river of My delights. With Me is the fountain of life, and in My light you see light" (Psalm 36:7, 8).

** I come to Jesus by the river and drink my fill. As a little child, I wade in and dip my hand and drink again and again. "More! You need more," Jesus says. Jesus dips and pours water over my head and laughs. I dip and drink more. "This is the river of My delights. Be filled with life and joy from Me."

Jesus walks me upstream to the waterfall, and we step up to it. "You need more!" He laughs and pulls me under the falling water. "My joy is your strength." Light shines from Jesus, and there are rainbows in the mist all around Him. "Be filled with My joy. Don't be somber! Rejoice in Me!" So I dance with Jesus in the waterfall. This makes Him so happy, and we laugh together even more.

There is More

Cast off Guilt

"My precious sweet child," Father says. "I am pleased with you. Guilt and condemnation never come from Me to you. There is no condemnation to those who are in Me. Cast it off. I always love you, Sweetness. Outward things, possessions and how things look in your house – these things are only temporary. Focus on the things which are not seen. Do not allow that 'monkey' of guilt and condemnation to climb on your back. Guilt, condemnation and shame are evil spirits."

Come As a Little Child

"I'm with you, Baby Girl, "Jesus says. "I love you. Rest in Me. I'm taking care of you, Sweetness. Come to Me now as a little child. Come closer."

**I come close to Jesus as a little child, and He picks me up, hugs me and strokes my hair. He places my head on His shoulder. "Rest in Me," He says. "Don't be anxious about your Mom and Dad. I'm taking care of them. Trust in Me with all your heart, and don't lean on your own understanding. In all your ways look to Me, and I will show you where to go and what to do. You are in a good place when you don't know what to do if you look to Me and trust Me to show you. Lean on Me."

I put my little arm around Jesus' neck and lean my head on His shoulder.

Jesus in the Kitchen

"I love you, Baby Girl. Come to Me now," Jesus says. "Walk with Me today. Precious One, draw near to Me in your heart."

There is More

**I come to Jesus as a little girl. He hugs me then and picks me up on His lap. "I'm thirsty," I say.

"You are thirsty. Come to Me and drink," Jesus says. "I'm the only One who can satisfy your thirst. Drink of the Holy Spirit from My hand. Drink till you're satisfied, then drink some more, and the overflow will bless others." Jesus carries me down into the water, dips a pottery tumbler into the water and hands it to me. I drink.

"More, Jesus," I ask. Jesus gives me another drink of the living water. The water is clear and sparkling and refreshing. Jesus carries me on His hip.

**I see Him bringing me to my housecleaning job as a little girl. In my vision, He carries me into the house and then into the kitchen. Jesus starts to clean the counters with me still on His hip. He puts soapy water in the sink. He hands me a rag, and He has one, too. Jesus is singing. We clean the counter, then the fridge. Then Jesus whirls me around and makes me laugh. "My joy is your strength. Keep in mind that I'm not just with you. I carry you. Rejoice in Me. Be happy as you work, and I will work with you and carry most of the load for this task. The responsibility is on Me, not you, if you keep the attitude of a little child. Be aware of My presence in their house as you go today. I will carry you through each task. It's not harder for Me to do the work while I carry you. It's a joy to Me to be with you, involved in every detail."

You Will See It

(Note: At this time we are on our driving trip back to Mexico. We decide to stop in Kansas City so we can visit International House of Prayer on Friday and Saturday.)

There is More

**"Listen, and I will speak to you, Baby Girl. I love you, Sweetness. You are Mine always and forever. Come close to Me now, Precious One." I crawl up on Jesus' lap, and He hugs me and strokes my hair. We're sitting on a rock by the river, and I can see the city of God far off. It's like purplish crystals, mountain shaped and bright, with a light of its own. I want to see the city up close. I can't see it very clearly at all.

"You will see it," Jesus says. "You will live in that city as part of My Bride, Beloved. Last night the girl next to you said you were stunningly beautiful. You are. She was seeing into your soul and spirit. Your spirit and soul are gorgeous. You are more beautiful than the most stunning model or actress. You have that quality in your spirit and soul that My heart beats for. I long to be near you, and I always want you with Me. Today there are people prepared to speak My words to you and John. I put it in your heart to come here."

(Later that day, in the House of Prayer, I am so blessed to find out that the young lady singing so beautifully at the piano is Misty Edwards and that she will be there at the big meeting tonight...)

You ARE Healed

"You asked me why you are not healed," Father tells me. "You <u>are</u> healed. I am your Healer, and I have touched you. My power goes into your neck, My healing power. That pain you feel is a lie. Be confident in My healing touch, and it will be manifest. Blessing, you are covered with blessing."

"Lord," I say, "show Me Your ways that I may know You, God. I want to see Your face, to behold Your beauty, to be with You. I want to dwell in Your secret place."

There is More

"I want to be with you," God answers. "To hear you say that you love Me is My desire. I love it when you come to Me. I love it that you allow Me to shine My light on you. Dance with Me, Sweetness."

I dance with Jesus here in the House of Prayer and in the Spirit.

Galloping Oh So Fast!

**Now I am on the horse with Him in my vision under the trees. We're galloping oh so fast. "Hang on," He says.

"Can I ask where we're going?" I ask. "Why so fast?"

"You are changing fast under the trees," Jesus says. "I brought you here to Kansas City today. I want you to cling to Me. Stay on My horse. Do you see that we are still under the trees? There are giants in the faith here, and you are passing through quickly."

In my vision, it seems like we are going uphill now, still very fast. Jesus turns and smiles at me. "You're coming with Me, learning how to ride with Me."

Home Again

Wow! It's amazing that it's December already! Time goes so fast! Yesterday was a long day (driving all the way from Matehuala to Morelos in Mexico), but it is so good to be home again. Rafaela made quesadillas for us. What a blessing. It's so good to sleep in our own bed in our little apartment here in Mexico. "Lord, would You please speak to me today?" I ask. "I call to You, and You will answer me. I come to You, Jesus. You have the living waters, the words of eternal life. Eternal life is knowing You. Show me Your ways that I may know You. You have the words of eternal life."

There is More

"I'm right here, Baby Girl," He answers. "I love you so much. I fill you with My love. Come sit on My lap. I know you like no other. You are created different from any other person. There is no one like you. You are unique and special, and My love for you is unique and special. I created you for such a time as this. I brought you and John here in My timing and for a reason, for a season and with a purpose. You will be amazed at what I can do in and through you."

My Very Own

"Draw near to Me, and I will draw near to you. I wait for you to come to Me. I am your Healer. The devil is a liar."

**Jesus is waiting for me with open arms. I come to Him as a little girl. He picks me up and holds me close and speaks softly. "This is what you need most, Baby Girl: to know that I love you. My blessing is on you to know who you are, My very own little girl. You are My little ewe lamb. You are My princess, My very own. You are the daughter of the King. Know who you are, and keep your eyes fixed on Me. You come to Me so you can know who you are and how very much I love you. You are Sweetness and Light. Your name comes from Me and from Father. You have asked, and My Father grants you according to the riches of Our glory, to be strengthened with power through My Spirit in your inner man, in your soul and spirit. Be strengthened, not by might nor by power, but by My Spirit. Receive My anointing that comes from within by My Spirit. Like the trees in Zechariah 4, being rooted and grounded in love, they produce oil for light (Eph. 3:15-17). Sweetness and Light, your light comes from My Spirit within, as your roots go deep into the soil of My love. You drink the water of My Spirit, you know My love, and your life yields fruit, the fruit of the Spirit. From that fruit comes oil for light to the world. You are the world's light. My children are the only light the world

There is More

has. Look at the mystery of the trees. You are like a tree planted by streams of water. Stay close to Me. Be rooted and grounded in Me and My love. Wisdom comes from knowing Me and My love. You yield your fruit in season, the fruit of the Spirit: love, joy, peace, patience, goodness, faithfulness, kindness, gentleness, and self control. Whatever you do prospers" (Psalm 1:3; Gal. 5:22-23).

Blood and Water

**I come to Jesus as a little girl and stand before Him. Liquid love pours out of Him onto me. It comes gushing out of His chest and arms and showers me. In my vision, it washes over me, warm, clear, red liquid love. It absorbs into me and warms me on the inside. I'm reminded how blood and water poured from Jesus' side.

Jesus takes me by the hand, and we walk by the river. We come to a rock, and Jesus sits down and picks me up and holds me, hugging me to His chest. "I love you, Baby Girl. Don't forget that I love you very much. My love fills you. Just be still and let Me hold you. I love you; you are Mine."

Jesus gets up and carries me, still holding me to His chest, my head on His shoulder. He rocks me gently as we walk up the river. "Yes," He assures me, "that's right; just rest in Me, and let Me carry you."

I sense this wonderful closeness as He walks, and my tears are flowing as He touches my heart. Jesus sings to me, "Precious, you are precious to Me. My love for you is great. I love these times when you draw near, and you can receive My love. I'm holding you; I'm loving you; I'm holding you in My arms."

There is More

A New Song

I sing to You a new song/ A new song of praise to You, my God

I sing to You a new song/ A song that flows out of my heart

I love You and I give You praise

I love You, I praise You from my heart

All glory goes to You/ all honor belongs to You

I sing praise/ I give You glory and honor

What can I say that will bless You Lord?

What can I sing that will touch Your heart?

I'll sing of my love for You/ I'll sing of Your love for me

For I am Yours and what a wonder that You are mine

How wonderful that I am Your child

How wonderful that You are my Dad

I can receive Your love and it fills me

I'm Glad to Serve You

"Call to Me, and I will answer you," God says. "Come to Me."

**I'm a little girl, and Jesus is far away. He waits for me by the river. I come to Him running. He picks me up in His arms and swings me around. I'm thirsty, so He stoops down and dips in the water and gives me a drink from His hand. "I'm glad to serve you, to take care of you. It's My delight." I'm still in His arms, and He lays His hand on

There is More

my chest. "I give you My peace. Rest in Me. You are very precious to Me, and I love you so much. You are a joy to Me, little Princess."

I sit on Jesus' lap, and He gives me a drink from His hand. It occurs to me that Jesus' hand is part of His body. In the scriptures, the people of God are His body. "Does that mean that You will use believers to teach me and bring me Your words?" I ask.

"Yes, other believers are part of My body. I use them to help you drink My words."

(I've been reading from great men of faith, Lester Sumrall, John G. Lake, Smith Wigglesworth.)

Ride With Me

**I'm on the horse as a young woman with Jesus. We're still on the path under the trees, going very fast. Through the trees to my left I can see the river. It sparkles here and there. We are going uphill now. "These giant trees are planted by streams of water, the water that flows from My throne. Remember how you have passed through a series of conferences, teachings, books and trainings in the past few years, and it all seems to go so fast? These are the trees and branches of the trees that you are passing under quickly to get to where I want you to go. I'm taking you. You have passed under many great giants of the faith very quickly. As you hang on to Me and stay on My horse, we will continue to move forward quickly. Ride with Me."

I Breathe On You

"Holy Spirit," I say, "I need You to fill me more; more of Your presence. Possess me. Fill me. Use me. Take control more, so I die to myself and live for You and Your purposes. I wait for You now."

There is More

"I breathe on you," God replies. "My Spirit is coming to fill the room you sit in."

**I see the glory like a spiral of sparkling cloud. God blows it into the room. It comes down to me where I sit in my chair; then it stops.

"Fill me with Your glory," I plead, "Your breath, Your Holy Spirit. Come in, envelope me, take control! I'm thirsty for You! Why do You stop, Holy Spirit? What do You need to do? Search me. Is something blocking the flow of Your Spirit?"

"Wait on Me," He says. "I will speak. Wait... If I do as you ask, you will be changed. Are you ready for that?"

"Yes, Lord," I reply. "Any change that You make will be good, even if it doesn't appear so to me. Fill me, please. I don't want to stay the same."

"Yes, stay here and wait," God says. "Wait 20 minutes more. Keep watch to see what I will speak to you and how to reply when you are reproved. Wait. Be still; focus on Me."

I see the breath of God coming from Him on the throne just above me. As He blows the wind of the Spirit and the cloud comes into the room, His hand also comes to comfort me. Father's hand is on my shoulder to steady me. I'm hearing the voices of the doves and birds outside my room; there's a rhythm to them, a beautiful sound.

"They praise Me," God says. "They are in My rhythm. Join in the chorus."

"Praise You, praise You," I sing along with the doves. "I give glory to God. Glory, glory, glory. I love You, I love You. The palm tree – its

There is More

leaves are swaying in the wind, and it glorifies You, God. Even the trucks and buses going by have their tune. "

"Baby Girl," God says, "keep in tune to the rhythm of LIFE. All life comes from Me. Let Me change you and rearrange you on the inside. Let Me change how you hear and see things."

There's More

"Lord," I say, "I keep thinking there's MORE. I have heard and read about so many of Your servants who have been touched by the power of Your Spirit in an overwhelming way, with shaking and fire. You touch and call them, and now they have a burning message to touch others in the same way. I want Your fire to burn in me. I want to be changed. I want a new baptism with Your Spirit. I know there's more of You, and I hunger and thirst for more. It grieves me that in my vision yesterday, the glory of Your Spirit came into the room, came close to me and then stopped. Fill me!"

"Those who hunger and thirst for Me will be filled," God says. "The pure in heart will see Me. Since you hunger and thirst, you will be satisfied. My glory is what you saw yesterday, My glory cloud. My Spirit is here in you, that's how you can hear My voice. But for My glory to fill you, even to touch you is another thing. Keep asking. One day you will be ready to receive it. I have shown you My glory. Yesterday you were hearing the sounds of creation with your spiritual ears. Keep asking. I give the Holy Spirit to those who ask. I am making you ready. It's because of mercy that I don't touch you and change you all at once. Yes, there is more. Keep asking for it, and trust Me."

There is More

It's My Mercy that My Glory Waits

"The best way to praise Me is to listen to Me," God says. "You honor Me by seeking My face, not by many words. Pay attention to Me, to what I say. Be ready to do what I tell you. It's when you hear My words and do them that you are wise. You are asking for more of Me. I am pleased with that request. Don't be distressed that My glory comes close but doesn't touch you. It's My mercy that My glory waits. I covered Moses with My hand so he would not die when My glory was passing by (Ex. 33:22, 34:5-6). That desire for more of Me, for My presence and My glory to touch you is a good desire. I am pleased. Wait on Me, and you will renew your strength."

Come to Me By the River

"Good morning, Sweetness," God says. "I love you, Baby Girl. Seek Me; seek My face. Let Me fill you with My love. Come to Me by the river."

**Jesus is standing by the river, waiting for me. I'm a little girl, and when I come close, His face lights up in a big smile. He takes my hands and squats down to my level. "Beautiful Baby Girl, I love you always. I'm so happy that you came when I called." He gives me a hug. "Walk with Me under the trees." He leads me to the edge of the wooded area where there are great trees, and we walk together, my hand in His.

Touch the Golden Scepter

"Good morning, Sweetness," God says. "It's My delight to spend time with you. I love you. I'm right here with you to pour out My Spirit on you. The same Spirit that raised Jesus from the dead dwells in you. I give life to you by My Spirit. I am your Healer. I gave you authority

There is More

over every kind of sickness. All life comes from Me. I am the giver of life."

**I can imagine myself coming near to the throne in heaven. I bow down before His feet. There is a bright light and rainbows and stars. God is light, and in Him is no darkness at all.

"Heaven," God says, "is closer than you think it is. Don't worry that you can't see clearly. In the world, you see as if through a glass darkly. Still, in the Spirit, you can come near. I hold out the golden scepter to you for you are a part of the Bride for My dear Son Jesus."

"Father," I say, "I come to You. My desire is to be with You where You are."

"You are here with Me," God says, "by faith. Believe it. My love for you is greater than you can imagine. Reach out in the Spirit and touch the golden scepter of My power."

I touch the end of the golden scepter, and I say, "Worthy are You, my Lord and my God, to receive glory and honor and power for You created all things, and for Your pleasure they are and were created" (Rev. 4:11). I notice there is a crown on my head. I take it off and lay it at the Father's feet. "All glory to You," I say, "Blessing and glory and honor and power and dominion forever and ever" (Rev. 5:13). All around are the crowns of the elders and the saints. "Holy, holy, holy," I join in with the angels and saints in worship. In my room, I bow down with my face to the floor and worship Him with passion and tears.

Keep Oil in Your Lamp; Night is Coming

I wake up two hours earlier than usual, and I hear God saying, "Come away beloved, give Me half an hour now."

There is More

It's all quiet except for the roosters, and they all seem to cry out, "It's a new day!"

"And God," I ask, "what do You want to say to me?"

"I'm blessed that you obeyed My voice," God says. "I know you really want to go back to sleep. I love you, and I am pleased that you came. I'll let you sleep in a while. Now, come up here, up to My throne."

**So here I am again at the feet of the Most Holy One. "Holy, holy, holy!" the angels and saints cry out.

"Come up here, and sit down," Father says. I come closer and see there's a throne for me. "Of course, there's a throne for you. You are a princess." An angel brings my crown to me and places it on my head. I'm wearing a white robe with a golden sash. Another angel brings me a blue satin cape with blue stones and diamonds set into it.

"Don't worry that you can't see clearly," God says. "You are here in the spirit none the less."

Jesus is on my left on His throne. "Today, you sit here spiritually representing My Bride," He says. "One day all of My Bride will be seated here. Keep oil in your lamp so you can shine for Me. Night is coming. This is a time when you can store up oil for light" (Matt. 25:1-13).

"Lord," I say, "I'm not really sure how to store up oil. I know the oil represents the Holy Spirit."

"Yes," Jesus says, "do as you have been doing, keep asking Me for more. The night is coming. When the night comes, you need not be in darkness. You are a child of light and of the day. Do not sleep as

149

others do, but be alert and sober (1 Thess. 5:1-11). "You are not in darkness, that the day would overtake you as a thief in the night. But I tell you, be ready. Be on guard so your heart will not be weighted down with the worries of life and that day will not come upon you suddenly like a trap. Keep on the alert at all times, praying" (Luke 21:34-36).

I look for and find the verses where Jesus said, "We must work the works of Him who sent Me as long as it is day; night is coming when no one can work. While I am in the world, I am the light of the world" (John 9:4-5).

"Now, you are the light of the world," Jesus says. "Shine for Me. Shine with My light" (Matt. 5:14,16).

My Little Crown

**I'm a little girl, sitting on Jesus lap, looking into His eyes. I put my little hands on both sides of His face, and He smiles at me. There's nothing like Jesus' smile. I put my little crown on His head. Jesus laughs, and He has such love in His eyes. He puts the crown back into my hands and gives me a hug. "I love you," He says. "You're My little girl, My princess."

His Face Shines with Love

**Jesus is standing with His arms outstretched, and He is shining. I come to Him, and I can feel the warmth radiating from Him, like standing in the sunshine. I kneel at His feet. Jesus puts one hand on my shoulder and the other hand on my head, and warmth goes into me. He lifts my head up so I can look into His face. His face shines with love. "Princess, stand up," He says. I stand, and He takes my hands. Then He gives me a hug, and I am warmed inside and out as

There is More

His love flows into me. There's a sparkling radiance around us, and as I step back, there's a glow around me, too. "Daughter of Light," He says, "let your light shine. Walk close to Me today, and you will shine for Me."

On Father's Lap

**I'm with Jesus, and He brings me near to the Father's throne in heaven. Jesus is holding my hand. "I'm with you. Don't be afraid," He says.

"Father," I say, "I want to see more clearly in the spirit realm. Touch my heart. I want to be closer to You in my day-to-day walk. I need healing in my body. You are everything, You are all important. I want to worship You in spirit and truth."

"The best way you worship," Father says, "is to listen to My voice. When you look to Me and to My son Jesus, and you depend on My Holy Spirit to teach you and guide you. You are worshipping Me in spirit and in truth. Wait for Me now."

I bow down with my face to the ground at Father's feet. Jesus lays His hand on my shoulder.

"It's alright, Daughter, that you can't see clearly," Father says. "Stay here awhile, Sweetness. Wait for Me. That's right; be still and wait...." I wait for a few minutes; then I hear Him say, "Come up here."

Jesus helps me to my feet, and then Father pulls me up on His lap. His arms are around me, and He gently guides my head so that it leans on His chest. My tears are really flowing. Something is being touched and healed deep inside me.

There is More

"Oh Father," I say, "change what needs to be changed inside me."

"Just stay here a while, and let Me love you," Father says. "My perfect love will do its perfect work. My love is what you need. Rest in Me and My love. Wait on Me. It will be worthwhile. I love you Precious One. I love you, Baby Girl. My love is enough and more than enough." In my vision, I'm curled up on Father's lap, and my head is on His chest. "Rest in Me; rest in My love. I love you, Daughter."

"I love You, Daddy," I say.

"In the spirit, you are here, and I'm really holding you," Father says. "You can come here whenever you want, and I will hold you and love you. I want you to receive My love so you can love others. Stay a little bit longer now. Spend time here, and you will be able to hear My heart. You will hear what I'm saying to others. You will tell those who can't hear Me for themselves."

Father Blows on Me

"Father," I say, "I come to You in Jesus' name. Yesterday, Jesus brought me to You, but then You said I can come to You any time. I come boldly to Your throne, because of Jesus who is my high priest" (Heb. 4:16).

**So I come to the throne and bow down and worship.

"Come here, Baby Girl," Father says. "Come up on My lap." I come, and He picks me up and puts me on His lap, His arms around me. "Daughter, I love you. You still need to know it more. Yes, you are in a battle, and the enemy has attacked you, but My Son Jesus has already won the victory. The enemy has not been allowed to harm you. My love strengthens you. You need more of My perfect love that casts out fear. Rest in Me and My love. I give you strength for

There is More

the battle. Don't be disappointed or dismayed. Rejoice in Me, I am the God who heals you."

I ask for the Holy Spirit to come and fill me more.

Father blows on me, "Be filled with My Spirit, My Spirit of love and joy and grace. You are a princess, and My Spirit fills you. I fill you with light."

I think I see the seven lights of flame around the throne, but it's not clear at all.

"Don't worry that you don't see clearly," He says. "You are learning, and I am showing you all that you need to see now. Go now in the strength of this moment, knowing that I hold you, and My Spirit fills you."

My Love is Fresh and Sweet

**I hear Jesus say, "Come to Me." I come to Jesus by the river, as a little child, and He hugs me. "You need My love most of all, Sweetness," He says. "You need to be made perfect in My love. Stay here with Me for a while, and listen to Me. I will teach you."

Jesus picks me up and carries me on His hip. We walk up river. It's a new day. The sun is just coming up. The birds are singing. We're walking on a dirt path next to the river. The river is about ten feet across here. Jesus brings me to a tree that's bearing fruit. It's a pomegranate tree. He picks a piece of fruit; it's perfectly ripe. He opens it, and inside the bright red fruit glistens in the sunshine. Jesus feeds it to me, and we eat it together. It's very sweet, and the seeds are soft and chewable. We keep walking up the path.

There is More

"Trust Me to feed you," Jesus says, "physically and spiritually. My words are sweet, pure and joyful. My words are very special, like perfectly ripe fruit. By My Spirit, you can know My thoughts. I reveal astounding truths to you by My Spirit (1 Cor. 2:9-16). I combine spiritual thoughts with spiritual words. I freely give you things which you have never thought of before; I give you My wisdom. You have eaten this with Me; I will share My thoughts with you as well."

"Lord Jesus," I ask, "what do You want to show me today? What do You want to share with me?"

"Today is a new day, like the light of dawn that shines brighter and brighter (Prov. 4:18). My love for you is fresh and sweet, like the fruit we shared. There's always more for you. My love for you is new every morning, fresh and sweet. You are on a path of discovery, and little by little I'm showing you things."

"Thank You for this, Lord, but I want more!" I plead. "I know there's much more than what I've been experiencing. There's a longing in my heart for more of Your glory and power, so more people will come to You because they know You are real. Do whatever it takes to change me, Lord. I'm desperate."

Jesus smiles, "As I said, there's always more for you. Today you are closer than you were yesterday, and you have eaten with Me. I am bringing you along the path that shines brighter and brighter. I'm teaching you and taking you where you need to go."

I'm thinking about the vision of Jesus and me on the horse going fast.

"Yes," Jesus says, "you have been listening to some giants in the faith. It is taking you where you need to go. You are still with Me on my horse. I have been speaking to your heart, Sweetness, and I will change you. I'm taking you to a place where you can receive what I have for you. It's a good prayer to pray that you allow me to do whatever it takes to change you, but there are things I want to do that you are not ready for yet."

"Oh, Lord," I say, "make me ready."

It's on my heart to read Smith Wigglesworth. I read his sermon on Jacob and his wrestling with God. Jacob's attitude was very similar to the desperation I'm starting to feel. "I won't let You go until You bless me," I say. "I can't go on without Your blessing. I'm lost without Your blessing. I'm lost without You, God. I'm desperate for You."

Come Closer

**"Come up here," Father says. I come up to the foot of His throne and bow down. I cast my crown at His feet. Jesus comes and lays His hand on my shoulder, then He helps me to my feet. An angel brings my crown to me and places it back on my head with much respect.

"Hello, Princess," Father says. "Come closer." I walk up to the Father's knees, and He takes my hand. "How much you've grown. You are such a beautiful young woman. You are starting to receive My love, and it makes you so beautiful. You need more, Daughter. Come here." He draws me up on His lap and hugs me. "My love will fill every need that you have or will ever have." He takes my crown and puts it on my lap, then lays my head on His chest. "Receive My love, Sweetness; receive more." *(In my vision, I'm about 25 years old.)*

I'm Not Restricted by Time

**I'm on Father's lap. My head is on His chest. "I feel much better today," I say. "Thank You for healing me…. Time goes so quickly."

There is More

"Yes," Father says, "for you it goes quickly, but remember that I don't dwell in time. I'm not restricted by time. On the earth you are confined to time and space, but in the Spirit, you're eternal and all things are possible. I can do a year's work in you in one moment. Here you are; spiritually, you are on My lap, and My arms are around you. My love is doing a work in your heart."

"Yes, Father!" I exclaim. "Do a work in my heart. Change me. Any changes You make will be very good."

"Rest in Me," Father says. "Rest. Now tell Me about anything that's troubling you."

"Should I go to see the doctor again?" I asks. "I feel a little fragile, and I don't want to hear any discouraging words." *(I have been battling an intestinal disorder for many months.)*

"You are not fragile," Father says. "You are strong in Me. My love strengthens you. Take authority over spirits of fear. Your strength is in Me and in My Spirit. Stay here and breathe the air of heaven. Let My love and My touch fill you. Drink in My love. I love you so much, more than you can imagine! My Spirit is with you every moment. Ask Me, and I will help you," Father says, and He breathes on me. His breath is a glory cloud, and it settles around me, sparkling with brightness. I breathe in the glory, and light goes into me.

Focus and Determination

**Jesus walks up the path by the river, but His back is turned to me. I'm a young girl, and I run after Him and call, "Jesus!" He stops, turns around and waits for me to come. When I get to Him, He picks me up and hugs me, laughing. Then He swings me around in a circle, and we laugh together.

There is More

"Call to Me, and I will answer you," He says. "I love you so much. I have great things for you. Stay here with Me for a little while. I have something to show you." Jesus takes me by the hand, and we walk along the path by the river. It's a bright beautiful day. We come to a little bush with red flowers by the side of the path. There's a little bumble bee going from flower to flower, gathering nectar and pollen. His back legs are packed full of the yellow pollen.

"Jesus," I ask, "why did You show me this? What do You want me to know about it?"

"I created that little bee," Jesus answers. "See how diligent he is. He keeps on working; he won't quit till he has visited every flower on this bush. Then he will go to other flowers till he can carry no more. He will take it back to his hive. Once he's dropped off his load, he will continue his searching and gathering. He has focus and determination."

I'm reminded of the verse, "One thing have I desired of the Lord, that will I seek after; that I may dwell in the house of the Lord all the days of my life, to behold the beauty of the Lord and to inquire in His temple" (Psalm 27:4).

"Exactly," Jesus says. "Keep your focus on the one thing. Your relationship with Me is the most important thing, the more excellent way. Like Mary, choose the good part, the more excellent way. Be like Mary. Focus on Me and your relationship with Me. Sit at My feet, and listen to what I have to say. Let it be more important than your service to others" (Luke 10:38-42).

"My presence in your life will simplify things for you." He says. "Keep your focus on Me, not just in the morning devotional time. But be

There is More

like this little bee, and gather honey from My mouth all day. Be determined, diligent and focused."

There's Always More of Me

In returning and rest, you shall be saved; in quietness and in trust shall be your strength (Isaiah 30:15). "Rest and wait," God says. "Watch to see what I will speak to you. Look to Me, and I will tell you all you are ready to hear, and I will show you all you are ready to see."

"Search me," I ask. "I'm sorry for not asking You what I should do when I had free time last night."

** I'm in the river with Jesus, and He pours water on me and washes me clean. "When I wash you," He says, "you are clean. Don't allow any guilt or condemnation to stay. I cleanse you from all unrighteousness. It's a new day, a new beginning, a fresh start. Tell Me now about what concerns you."

I pray for my son David who needs a job. "Jesus," I say, "your word says my descendants are a blessing, and they will be mighty on the earth" (Ps.37:27, Ps.112:2). I talk to God about other things, then I say, "I want more of You, more of Your glory, more of Your Spirit in me."

"There's always more of Me," God says. "I'm infinite."

I sing in tongues and dance for a few minutes. I feel like I'm in heaven dancing with saints and angels. I'm pretty sure that the chorus I'm singing -- "Kuri, kuri, kuri" -- means "Holy, holy, holy."

Now I hear God singing over me:

There is More

I SING OVER YOU

I sing over you, I sing over you

With songs of joy and songs of love

I sing over you, for you are My child

You bring Me joy, you bring Me love

And your love, it pleases Me

It brings joy to My heart

So I sing over you; you are My child

Open to Me, Beloved

"I'm right here with you," Jesus says, "right here. Listen to Me now for a little while. You need Me more than you know. I Am your Healer. I love you so much. Open to Me, Beloved."

"What do I need to do to open up to You?" I ask. "As much as I can, I do. I open my heart to You. I give my life to You. My life is Yours. I hear Your voice, and I open the door. You promise to come in to me and dine with me, and I will dine with You (Rev. 3:20). Come in, Lord."

Jesus Dines with Me.

****Jesus is by the river. I'm with Him as a little girl about nine years old. There's a little table with a simple white cloth on it and two chairs. An angel brings two plates and two each of forks, knives, spoons and cloth napkins. I help set the table. Another angel brings a basket of bread and a pitcher of clear, red juice and two crystal glasses. Jesus pours and says, "Sit down." As I sit down, another

There is More

angel brings a tray with broiled fish and a dish of vegetables, setting them on the table. Jesus serves my plate, then His, and He sits down.

"Thank You, Jesus," I say.

The little table is by the river, under the shade of a big tree. The sun shines, and birds sing in the trees. A soft breeze blows. The angels are gone now; it's just Jesus and me. Jesus opens the napkin from the bread, and He tears the flat bread in half, handing half to me and keeping the other. "Thank You, Jesus," I say. I'm wondering if I should thank Father for the food, and I'm waiting to see what Jesus will do. Jesus just smiles at me. "I'm so thankful," I say, "to You and to Daddy God, that I can sit here with You and enjoy a meal with You. Thank You!" Jesus nods, and we start to eat. The food is simple but delicious.

Jesus says, "Tell Me about the things that concern you."

So I talk to Jesus about the things that are in my heart.

"You are just a girl," Jesus says. "Have you been trying to figure these things out on your own? Don't you know that I care about you and want to help you? Be sure to talk to Me about whatever concerns you."

Key to My Healing

(Note: this is the day I received a breakthrough on my healing. I had been suffering from intestinal problems for more than eight months. These scriptures God ministered to me were the key to my complete healing.)

"I'm right here with you and in you," God says. "I work things together for good for you. I Am your Healer. You can trust Me."

There is More

"Lord," I answer, "I trust You with all my heart. Forgive me if I have been leaning on my own understanding. Forgive me if I have been wise in my own eyes by going to the doctor and trying to figure this out. I confess and repent. You promise to cleanse me from ALL unrighteousness (1 John 1:9). I fear You and turn away from evil. It will be healing to my body and refreshing to my bones" (Prov. 3:5-8).

"Daughter," God says, "listen to Me and My words. Tune in to what I say. I say I love you, and I Am your Healer. My perfect love fills you and casts out fear. Watch over your heart with all diligence, for from your heart flow the springs of life. My words are life to you and health to your <u>whole</u> <u>body</u>. Do you believe it? Focus on My words, what I say about you. I heal all your diseases (Psalm 103:3).

"You speak faith to others when you minister. Speak to yourself, as well. Put away from you a deceitful mouth, and put devious speech far from you. Look to the path ahead – the path of complete health and healing and wholeness. Watch the path of your feet and all your ways will be established" (Prov. 4:20-27).

I Know There's More

"Lord, I want more!" I cry out to God, "I know there's more of You. Do whatever it takes in me, but I need more. I am hungry for You, for Your Spirit, and for Your GLORY."

"Listen to Heidi Baker today," Jesus says. "Keep walking with Me under the trees. Ride with Me under the trees. I will take you where you need to go. Hang on to Me. Hang on to My horse."

(I have been listening to Sid Roth's programs over the internet. I recommend his radio program "Messianic Vision" and television

There is More

program "It's Supernatural". The archives of past shows are on the internet at www.sidroth.org, and you can listen for free.)

Yes, There's More

"My heart's cry is for more," I pray, "more of Your Spirit, more of You, more of Your glory. Let heaven come to earth in my life, LORD. I'm hungry and thirsty."

"You are thirsty; come to the waters. You're hungry; come buy and eat (Isaiah 55:1). I Am the bread of life; I have the words of life for you."

** I come to Jesus by the river. Jesus hugs me, and we wade into the river so I can drink. Jesus gives me a drink from His hand. I'm a small girl. I drink again and again. The water is refreshing. "My words are what you need most. Look at what you need most. Look at what I spoke to your heart last Thursday" *(see Key to My Healing, page 161).*

I re-read this, and then I say, "Jesus, fill me more. I'm hungry. I know there's more. Forgive me if I haven't trusted You as I ought. Thank You for being my Healer. Lord, I need Your words; please speak to me."

"Patty," Jesus says, "it's true that you need to change in order to receive what I have for you. Wait on Me. Keep asking. Listen and wait, and you will be filled."

"Today? Could I please have more of You today?" I plead. "Could You change me, rearrange me? Make me ready, or show me what I still need to do."

There is More

"Look at Isaiah 55," Jesus says. "Seek Me while I may be found; call upon Me while I am near (vs. 6). I am near. I'm right here in the river. You are with Me."

"I thank You that I can find You," I answer. "You are good and loving, but I know there's more."

**Jesus places His hands on either side of my face and smiles with such love in His eyes. "Yes," He says, "there's more." Then He blows gently on my face. I breathe in. I want to hold the breath of God. "Trust Me," Jesus says. "Didn't I tell you that I am taking you where you need to go? We are going quickly. You are on My horse; we are passing under the trees very fast. This is why your hunger and thirst for Me are growing. You will be filled – stay on My horse, under My trees. Yesterday, as you listened to Heidi and Roland Baker, it whetted your appetite for more. You are getting closer, but we still have a way to go. Keep asking. Keep reading and listening to the giants in the faith, and soon you will be filled with more of Me."

I read two sermons of Smith Wigglesworth, and they also whet my appetite, making me realize how hungry I am. I'm hungry and thirsty for more of God's Spirit and for my eyes to be opened that I can see what God wants me to see. "Open my eyes!" I cry out. "I need more, God, more Holy Spirit."

You Need More of My Love

"Lord, I need more of You, more of Your love, more of Your Spirit. Only You can satisfy the longing in my heart. Show me Your ways that I may know You! O, that I may know You and find favor in Your sight. Father, thank You for this room, that I can have this time alone with You. I come up to Your throne now. Your word says I can come boldly before Your throne, because Jesus is my high priest who goes

There is More

before me. If there's any sin, search me and know my heart; cleanse me, O God. Wash my feet; they get dirty from walking in this world. Thank You, Jesus, for paying for it all."

"Be still now, and wait on Me," God says. "Those who wait on Me will renew their strength. Your strength in Me will be renewed."

**Jesus is beside me, and He helps me to stand before Father's throne. Jesus puts His arm around my shoulders.

"You want to know Me," Father says. "Come closer." I step closer, and Father lifts me up on His lap and lays my head on His chest. "Knowing My love more is the most important thing you need. You need more of My love. My love makes you secure. My love casts out fear. My love is all you need and more than you need. My love will satisfy that longing in your heart. I love you, Precious One. You are very special and precious to Me. I have such plans for you. To fulfill these plans, you need more of My love. My love will satisfy your thirsty soul. My love will satisfy your hunger. Let My love fill you. My love is forever. I always love you, always have and always will. My love is constant and consistent. I have loved you with an everlasting love, therefore I have drawn you with loving-kindness (Jer. 31:3). I loved you long before you were born, and I love you now. I made you especially for the time and place in which you live. I shower you with My love and blessing. Be filled to overflowing with My love. I love you."

I Reveal Things You Never Thought of Before

"I'm here, Baby Girl," Jesus says. "Come to Me."

**I come to Jesus as a little girl, four or five years old. Jesus stoops down to give me a hug, then picks me up in His arms and twirls

There is More

around, making me laugh. "I love you," He says. "You are a bright light, Patty. Shine for Me. Don't be afraid to shine, do not hide your light. My love shines through your eyes. My love fills you and casts out fear. Peace and rest come with My love, Sweetness. Look for My words, My special rhema words for you as you read the scripture today. I have something special for you. Write it down. There is great treasure in My word."

"Through My Spirit, I reveal things you never thought of before; things no one has ever thought of," He says. "My Spirit searches the depths of Me. I could reveal something to every man, woman and child on the planet, something no one has ever thought of before, something new every day for their whole lives and not run out. I have special thoughts just for you. I want you to know them. My heart rejoices in you, because you want to hear, you want to know Me more" (1 Cor. 2:9-10).

"Lord," I ask, "what would You reveal to me today? Is there something You want me to know or to have? Your word tells me, 'All things belong to you' (1Cor. 3:21) and You 'freely give us all things' (Rom. 8:32) and the Spirit helps us to 'know the things freely given to us by God' " (1 Cor. 2:12).

"What things then do You freely give me today?" I ask.

"I give you My love, new for today," God says. "I give you a new day, a new song." Then God sings over me,

"I sing over you with a new song

A song of My love and My joy

I rejoice over you with love in My heart

There is More

I rejoice over you for you are My child

I sing over you with a new song

You are precious, you are lovely

You are Sweetness, you are Light

My heart sings to you; My heart sings to you, My child

"You may think that I have sung this song to someone else, but I have not," God says. "It's new, just for you. And this is a new day just for you. No one has ever walked the same paths that you will walk today. No one else has the same plan that I have for you. You are unique and special. I have been preparing you for this day, a special day. Rejoice in this special day that I have given you. No one else is qualified to be you today! You have a very special role."

Tell Them, "It is Finished"

**I come to Jesus as a little girl. He holds me in His arms. "I want to fill you with My love, Baby Girl. Receive My love now."

I see His love go into me, clear, red liquid love. It comes right out of His chest and into mine. I feel it filling me, and I remember how blood and water poured out of His side when He was pierced. It makes me cry with a sweet sadness, but it also feels warm.

"I love you enough to die for you. I love you enough to leave My throne in heaven with all its glory. I left all the light and love and worship of heaven to come and rescue you, and I would do it all again if needed, but the work is finished. Everything was completed for your salvation and healing. My Bride just needs to receive what is already bought and paid for. Tell them. Tell them that when I said, **'It is finished,'** it really was. Tell them today." (John 19:30, 34)

There is More

Vision: Stick, Stone, Leaf

"I'm here with you," God says. "I'm always with you, watching over you, yet I wait for you to come to Me, to turn your attention to Me. Come to Me now. Quiet yourself. Be still, and listen to Me. Let My peace rule in your heart. Come to Me by the river." (I am having trouble being still today. I keep getting up. Finally, I shut the door to my room and sit very still in my chair.)

**I come to Jesus as a little child. Jesus is squatting down by the edge of the stream. He has a stick in His hand, and the stick is in the water, and we watch the water flow over and under it. Jesus puts His other arm around me and strokes my hair affectionately. "Look how fast the river is flowing," Jesus says. He takes a leaf from the bank of the river, and tosses it into the current. We watch as the leaf is carried quickly downstream. Jesus hands a leaf to me, and I toss it in. It whirls and twirls a little and then quickly floats down the stream and out of sight.

"Lord Jesus," I ask, "what do You want me to know about this?"

"You can be like a stick in My hand," Jesus replies, "or like a leaf or like a stone submerged in My river."

I notice the stones in the river, all rounded and smoothed. "What am I like?" I ask.

"Sometimes," Jesus answers, "you are like a precious stone; part of My spiritual house. Sometimes you are like a useful stick in My hand with the river flowing under and over you, and other times you are like a leaf, floating freely in My living water, letting My Spirit carry you as He will. But always stay close to My river. Let My Spirit teach you, wash you, carry you. Be secure and know that even as a leaf

There is More

floating in My river, you have significance and importance. See how the leaf demonstrates how fast the river flows." Jesus takes another leaf and tosses it in, and we watch it. "Others will see the effects of My Spirit on your life."

Jesus takes the stick and reaches down to the rocks in the river and moves them around. "You can be like this stick in My hand. I use you to move people and awaken them to My purpose. As you yield to Me, I will use you more, for My purposes." Jesus uses the stick to dig a little channel in the sandy shore area next to the river, and right away water from the river flows into the little channel. It washes away some sand to reveal some round river stones. "I can use you," Jesus says, "to bring My river, My living water to those who have moved away from the stream. See how My living water washes over them and they are brightened. Before, they had buried themselves in the sand. You can help to awaken people to their calling and to the power of My Spirit."

Jesus reaches into the deeper water and pulls out a round river stone. The stone is blue like my stone in the spiritual house. "You can be like this stone, submerged in the river of My Spirit. As the water washes over it, it bumps against the other stones and wears them smoother, and the stone itself gets smoother. Don't worry about it when it seems that My Spirit leads you in a way that rubs against others. It's all to My purpose. Only smooth stones are part of My spiritual house which represents My city and My Bride. I'm coming for My Bride without spot or wrinkle or any such thing. You can help others to become part of My Bride, pure and spotless, smooth and polished."

There is More

Everyone Needs a Touch Every Day

**I come to Jesus by the river, He has the stick in His hand, and He's stooped over, touching the river rocks with His stick. When I come to Him as a little girl, He hugs me, and then He keeps touching different stones in the river like He's counting them. I watch as the stick touches each stone, and I'm wondering what He's doing.

"Are You counting stones?" I ask.

"No," Jesus answers, "I'm touching them. I can use this stick of wood to touch them. Every one of them needs a touch from Me every day. You are a stone in My river, and I use others to touch you. You are a stick in My hand, and I use you to touch others. My river of My Holy Spirit washes you and makes you clean and fit for My use."

I Want to Help You With Everything

"I want to know You more," I plead with God. "I need more of You. Draw me closer, oh Father. Holy Spirit, please fill me more. I know there's more. I'm thirsty for You."

"Come to Me," Father says.

**I'm trying to see myself before the throne, but something is blocking my vision today.

"It's okay that you don't see much," Father says. "Just listen to My voice. I love you, My child, My daughter. Princess, you are very precious to Me. I love you, I love you, I love you. Receive My love. I know that sometimes it's hard for you to hear My voice, but be assured that I am speaking. You do hear from Me. I want to help you with EVERYTHING. Include Me in all that you do. Listen for My voice. I am with you. With Me, one day is like a thousand years, and a

There is More

thousand years is like one day (II Peter 3:8). I can do more in one day that you could do in 1000 years. If you listen to Me and you obey Me, you step into My kingdom where time is totally different. I can do more with you in one day than you can imagine. I see the end from the beginning, and I want you to see part of what I see. I have been showing you visions of My will, what I want to happen. When you pray for people and I give you a vision, you can say a few words describing the vision; and it will have greater impact than thousands of words, because they will remember it. In this way, time is compressed or utilized to greater capacity because of lasting impact. I can do more in a minute or two than you could do in a year. Stay connected to Me, and you will redeem or save the time. Spend time with Me in the secret place. I will give you wisdom and insight about how to do everything better."

Afterword

Chapter 14

Afterword

(Even as this book is being edited and prepared for printing, the Lord is impressing on me to add some visions He has recently revealed. In every one, I see myself as a little girl in Jesus' arms and Him in the river where the water is deep. God has told me to put myself in the position of one of these visions when praying for others or when speaking to a group of people. This section is included here for you who have a desire to bless others. You, too, will find it helpful to see yourself so supported and embraced by Jesus as you minister.)

** Jesus is waiting for me in the river. He's in the water up to His thighs. I come as a young child. I start to wade in, but the water is too deep for me, so Jesus comes and picks me up. He gives me water to drink from His hand. He hugs me and kisses my cheeks, then gives me more water. The water is sweet and refreshing, just what I needed. "Don't worry about anything," Jesus says. "I'm with you. I'm your Provider. Be a little child in My arms. Haven't I always cared for you?"

"Yes, Jesus," I answer. "Of course, You have."

"I will never leave you nor forsake you. I will take care of you and John. Do not be worried about what you will eat or drink, nor for your clothes or for a car (Matt. 6:25). But seek first My kingdom and My Father's kingdom and My righteousness, and all these things will be added to you. So do not worry about tomorrow (Matt. 6:33-34).

Afterword

You are right in coming as a little child to Me. Keep looking to Me, and I will care for you."

Let Me Carry You *(I was prayed for at a healing conference, a prayer of impartation. The power of God touched me, and I fell to the floor. As I lay there, I received from the Lord.)*

"I love you," Jesus says. "I have such plans for you. I will lead you as you surrender to Me. Yield your life to Me, and lean back in My arms. I will take you where you need to go."

**Jesus picks me up and carries me, walking in the stream, walking upriver. We walk under the waterfall, and the water blasts us. Then Jesus climbs up to the top, still carrying me. "I'm taking you closer to My throne and Father's throne where this river originates."

I'm standing now, and the river is flowing out of my belly and people are coming to me for refreshing. It's like I'm standing in the river, and the water flows in and out of me. I see myself praying over people, and words of refreshing come out of my mouth – rivers of living water (John 7:38). Life flows out of my mouth.

Jesus carries me higher yet. "Let Me carry you," He says. "If you let Me carry you, you will arrive much faster, and we will have success. Lean back, and let Me carry you. I am able, but you must listen and yield. I have great plans for you. I will show you and lead you if you let Me carry you."

(Next day) Sweetness, you are a light in the darkness. My light shines from you, and words of life come from your mouth. I will use you today to bless many. You are blessed to be a blessing. Lean back, and let Me carry you. If I carry you, the light that is in Me shines though you. Lean back, and rest in My arms as you did in your vision

Afterword

yesterday. Do not strive. Rest in Me and in My goodness and strength. My Spirit leads you. I am holding you and helping you. Stillness, quietness and confidence will help you. Keep focused on Me. I love you so much, Baby Girl. Wait now in My arms and rest. Lean into Me."

**I'm a little girl about three, and Jesus is holding me. I lean my head on His shoulder. "That's right," He says. "I have strong shoulders, and I love you. If you stay right here in My arms, I will take care of everything. You don't have to work at making decisions about what to do or where to go next. Just stay in My arms and rest on My shoulder, and I will take you where you need to go. I love you. I know what you need and what you need to do. See yourself like this whenever you do anything, and I will be working in you and through you. You'll hear My voice saying, 'This is the way; let's go over here.' Then let Me take you there. Depend on My Holy Spirit, and lean on Me. Rest in Me like a little toddler. Be a little toddler. Stay close to Me. Smile, laugh and play.

An Impartation from Jesus *(The next day during prayer at the conference, Jesus touches me again.)*

**Jesus is carrying me in the river. I'm a little girl of two or three. The water is deep and running fast, way too deep and too strong a current for a little child to walk in. As Jesus walks, He lays His hand on my chest several times. Each time I feel more of His strength coming into me; it's an impartation from Jesus. He also blows on my face, and I breathe in the breath of God.

Afterword

Lean Back in My Arms

"Lean back in My arms, Baby Girl. I love you. Let Me carry you. I'm glad to carry you. I am strong. Lean back and rest in Me, and My strength will go through you. Be content to lean back and look into My face. Don't anxiously look around you. Look to Me. I am your Healer."

** I'm a little girl about three, and I lean back in Jesus' arms and look into His face. There is such love in His eyes. "I love you," He says and lays His hand on my chest. "Life! I came that you might have life and have it in abundance. Lean back and let Me impart My strength to you." Jesus is walking in the river, carrying me. the river narrows and deepens, up to Jesus' thighs, and then to His waist. As I lean back in His arms like a little baby, Jesus continues to lay His hand on my chest, and I am strengthened. As He touches my chest, waves of peace, power and warmth come into me. I am strengthened and have a sense of great security and contentment. Then He blows on my face.

"I can breathe the air of heaven," I sigh.

"Precious One, this is what you need: My love and My strength. I fill you with My strength and My anointing fills you. From this position, you can reach out and touch people when you pray for them. I am able to use you in a greater way when you keep in mind your own helplessness. Be sure to see yourself in this position whenever you minister. Be totally dependent on Me. Lean back in My arms as a little child, receive the impartation of My power and breathe the air of the breath of My Spirit. Do this, and I will give you what you need when you need it. I will take you where you need to go in the river of My Spirit."

Afterword

My Words are a Mighty River

"Lord, I'm thirsty for You," I say. "I'm thirsty for Your words of life."

**"Come to Me by the river," Jesus says. I go to Jesus as a little girl. He picks me up and hugs me, then walks right into the river. The water is rushing here up to His thighs. He dips in the water and brings His hand to my mouth so I can drink.

"My words are Spirit and life to you; drink."

I drink, and the water is so good and refreshing. "More please," I ask.

Jesus dips His hand again, and I drink. "Wait for My words; they are My Father's words, as well. Wait here in My arms."

I wait a little while, and Jesus says, "Do you see that here the river is rushing and too deep for you to stand in? My words are like this. I have so many things to tell you, but you must come as a little child to hear them. You can't do this on your own. You must be in My arms, surrendered to Me. Then you can hear what I'm saying. When you read My word, could you see yourself in this place first? My words are a mighty river. If you plunge in alone, you could drown or flounder or get washed downstream. Make sure you're with Me when you open My word. Don't lean on your own understanding."

"OK, Jesus," I answer. "I see. I've been trying to study Your word on my own. Is there anything else You want me to know before I go to Your word today? Open my eyes that I may see wondrous things in Your word. Please anoint my ears to hear what You are saying."

Jesus smiles and takes a little jar out of His pocket. He's still holding me, still in the river. He opens the jar and dips His finger in the ointment and then smears it on and in both of my ears.

Afterword

"Thank You, Jesus! What about my eyes?"

Jesus puts the ointment back in His pocket. He spits on His fingers, then touches my two eyes with the saliva. "Be opened!" He says with a smile. I love Jesus' smile even though I can't really clearly see it. When He smiles, His whole face lights up, and His teeth are so white!

The River of My Spirit is Powerful

I'm a little girl with Jesus by the river. The river is very powerful here and rushes over huge rocks in white-water rapids. The rapids are about eight feet tall and about 50 feet wide. Jesus picks me up, carrying me as you would a baby with one arm under my body and one under my head and arms. I'm leaned back in His arms, and Jesus walks right into the base of these falls. The power of the flow would knock any ordinary man over and carry him downstream, but Jesus is **strong. There are huge rocks under us, and Jesus steps from rock to rock, climbing higher and carrying me, holding me tightly. At the top, He sits down in about two feet of rushing water. The water courses so fast that Jesus has to hold me very tight so the river doesn't carry me away. The full force of the water rushes over my body. He holds only my head above water, but it's totally sprayed, as well. We are both completely wet. The water splashes and sprays as it hits us.

"Let Me take you here in the Spirit," Jesus says. "The river of My Spirit is powerful. You cannot come here unless I carry you, and even I cannot carry you here unless you come as a little child. Come as a little child, and let Me take you here when you need a new baptism in **the power of My Spirit**."

About the Author

Patty Schmid and her husband John are from St Paul, Minnesota. They have been missionaries with World Indigenous Missions since 1998, when they sold their home and left their jobs in Minnesota. Patty was a dental hygienist, and John a data base administrator. They moved south with their two young sons to prepare for missions in Mexico. After serving as missionaries for six years in Cuernavaca, Morelos, Mexico, they returned to Minnesota to help their sons establish their own lives in the USA. Since then, they also volunteer with International Association of Healing Rooms and have opened two Healing Rooms locations in St. Paul, Minnesota, where they continue to serve as directors. They now divide their time between the two countries, spending winters in Mexico and summers in Minnesota. In Mexico, they help to train Healing Rooms directors and team members and are excited to see so many miraculous healings and salvations through this powerful ministry.

You may contact Patty at patty_schmid@yahoo.com

Made in the USA
Charleston, SC
06 March 2012